P9-DWM-951

BUON APPETITO, YOUR HOLINESS

BUON APPETITO, YOUR HOLINESS

The Secrets of the Papal Table

MARIANGELA RINALDI
AND MARIANGELA VICINI

Translated from the Italian by
Adam Victor

ARCADE PUBLISHING • NEW YORK

Copyright © 1998 by Publigold s.r.l. - Milano
Translation copyright © 2000 by Macmillan Publishers Ltd.

All rights reserved. No part of this book may be reproduced in any form or by any electronic or mechanical means, including information storage and retrieval systems, without permission in writing from the publisher, except by a reviewer, who may quote brief passages in a review.

FIRST NORTH AMERICAN EDITION

Originally published in 1998 as *Buon Appetito Santità* by Publigold, Italy
This translation first published in Great Britain 2000 by Macmillan Publishers Ltd.

Library of Congress Cataloging-in-Publication Data

Rinaldi, Mariangela.
Buon appetito, your holiness : the secrets of the Papal table / Mariangela Rinaldi and Mariangela Vicini; translated from the Italian by Adam Victor.
p. cm.
Includes bibliographical references and index.
ISBN 1-55970-557-4
1. Cookery, Italian. 2. Popes. 3. Papacy—History. I. Vicini, Mariangela.
TX723 .R5274 2000
641.5945—dc21 00–57608

Published in the United States by Arcade Publishing, Inc., New York
Distributed by Time Warner Trade Publishing

Visit our Web site at www.arcadepub.com

10 9 8 7 6 5 4 3 2 1

EB

PRINTED IN THE UNITED STATES OF AMERICA

To Elio and Carlo

FELLOW PILGRIMS IN OUR LIVES

CONTENTS

LA CUCINA DEL PAPA

✞

Co la cosa ch'er coco m'è compare
m'ha vvorzuto fa vvéde stammattina
la cuscina santissiama. Cuscina?
Che cuscina! Hai da dì pporto de mare.

Pile, marmmitte, padelle, callare
cossciotti de vitella e de vaccina
polli, ova, latte, pessce, erba, porrcina,
caccia, e ggni sorte de vivanne rare.

Dico: "Prosite a llei, sor Padre Santo."
Disce: "Eppoi nun hai visto la dispenza,
che de ggrazzia de Ddio sce n'è antrettanto."

Dico: "Eh, scusate, povero fijjolo!
Ma ccià a ppranzo collui quarch'Eminenza?"
"Nòo," ddisce, "er Papa maggna sempre solo."

Giuseppe Gioacchino Belli

THE POPE'S KITCHEN

✞

My old mate the cook
this morning let me take a look
at the most holy kitchen. Kitchen?
What a kitchen! More like a seaport.

Piles of food, pots, pans,
great jars of veal and beef,
chickens, eggs, milk, fish, herbs, pork,
game and all kinds of rare dishes.

I said: "Your very good health, Holy Father."
He said: "Well, you should see the larder,
it's just as full by the grace of God."

I said: "Excuse me, my poor lad!
But is some great Eminence dining with him?"
"No," he said, "the Pope always dines alone."

A PONTIFICAL GLOSSARY

ABBOT: a title of high office, introduced by the first doctors of the Church. Today it is generally applied to anybody who wears the habit, particularly the superior of a monastery. Abbeys are so called in reference to the person in charge.

BISHOP: from the Greek *episkopos* (inspector, keeper). In the Catholic Church bishops have full powers of apostolic office in the preaching of the faith, the arrangement and conducting of worship, and the government of the ecclesiastic community.

BULL: an important pontifical document, tied up with red laces and fastened by a lead seal (*bolla* in Italian) bearing the mark of the keys of St. Peter.

CARDINAL: from the late Latin *cardinalis,* the adjective of *cardo*, hinge. As a noun, it is the title given to each of the seventy prelates who assist the pontiff and have a say at the conclave, the hinge on which the Catholic Church turns.

CONCLAVE: from the Latin *cum* (with) and *clavis* (key); formerly the room in which the cardinals were locked until they elected the Pope. Today it is the assembly of cardinals conducting the election.

CONSISTORY: a solemn meeting of cardinals convened by the Pope. The word also refers to the location where the assembly is held.

COUNCIL: from the Latin *concilium* (assembly), this is a meeting (national, provincial, diocesan, ecumenical) to which all the bishops of the Church are invited, as council fathers, to resolve fundamental issues regarding the faith or issues affecting society.

CROSIER: a long stick with curved handle like a shepherd's crook, the sign of episcopal dignity, carried in the left hand during solemn ceremonies.

ECCLESIASTIC: belonging or referring to the Christian Church, as opposed to lay or secular.

ECUMENICAL: from the Greek *oikoumenikos* (regarding the inhabited world). When combined with the word "council," it takes on the meaning "universal"; in other words it goes beyond the divisions between different Christian denominations, and aspires to achieve recovery of common values of faith. Catholic ecumenicalism developed after Vatican Council II, and after Pope John XXIII set up a secretariat for Christian unity.

ENCYCLICAL: from the Greek *en* (in) and *kyklos* (circle, ring). This is a document written by the Pope to clarify particular points of dogma or of ecclesiastical discipline and dispatched to all bishops around the world.

EXCOMMUNICATION: exclusion from communication with the faithful and from the sacraments, in accordance with the canons laid down by top Church hierarchy. This is the punishment authorized by canon law, inflicted only on individuals for grave moral reasons.

INDULGENCE: from the Latin verb *indulgere,* meaning to pardon. Indulgence may be granted after confession, though the after-death punishment of purgatory remains for serious sins. In some cases, after following special religious practices such as taking part in Jubilee rites, plenary indulgence may be obtained. In the sixteenth century, the so-called scandal of selling indulgences sparked off the Protestant Reformation.

JUBILEE: from Church Latin *jubileum,* itself derived from the Hebrew *jobel,* meaning ram, and indirectly horn-trumpet, because the sound of wind instruments made out of ram's horn. A Jubilee, which occurred every fifty years, heralded the beginning of a year of remission from debt, of the return of sold land to its previous owners and the freeing of slaves. In a Jubilee year in the Catholic Church, the supreme pontiff grants extraordinary plenary indulgence to the universal Church, with the right for all priests to absolve even reserved cases and to give absolution in exchange for simple votive offerings. Boniface VIII (1294–1303) decreed that the Jubilee should fall every hundred years; Nicholas V (1447–1455) reduced this interval to fifty years; Paul II (1464–1471) made it twenty-five, and so it has remained ever since.

MITRE: tall headgear split at the top into two peaks with

ribbons or strips dropping down the back. A mitre is worn by bishops and high prelates at ceremonies as a mark of authority and high office.

MONSIGNOR: the title for bishops, archbishops and ecclesiastics on whom special high office is bestowed. In the past it was used to address people of eminent high office, such as emperors, Popes, heirs to the throne and princes.

PILGRIM: from the late Latin *pelegrinus* or *peregrinus* (stranger), from which comes the verb "peregrinate," to travel or stay in foreign lands. A pilgrim is one who travels to other countries or one who visits holy sites for devotional reasons.

PONTIFF: from the Latin *pontifex,* which in the language of ancient Rome meant the highest religious authority and high priest, sometimes followed by the adjective *maximus.* Pontiff literally means "he who builds the bridge" [between earth and heaven], from *pons* (bridge) and *facio* (make, build).

PONTIFICAL MASS: a High Mass celebrated by the pontiff with the *Urbi et Orbi* blessing, or by bishops and abbots delegated to pass on the Pope's blessing to the faithful.

POPE: head of the Catholic Church and high priest, the Vicar of Christ on earth. The word derives from the Greek *papas,* meaning father. In Italian, *Papa* means Pope and, also, father.

PRELATE: from the Latin *praelatus* (person in charge), the proper title for the principal high priests such as cardinals, bishops and abbots. Prelates of the pontifical court have the right to wear violet.

ROMEO: the name given to pilgrims traveling to Rome, *caput mundi,* to visit the tomb of apostles Peter and Paul.

SEPTIZONIUM: ancient Roman ruin, a kind of fortress, in which the cardinals held the first conclave in history, at which they nominated Pope Innocent III (1198).

STAFF: the curved walking stick of the pilgrim, from which the water gourd was traditionally hung. The Italian term *bordone* derives from *burdo*, Latin for mule. To clutch the staff, for a pilgrim, was like hanging on to an obstinate and hardy mule.

THRONE: originally a high-backed rectangular seat with solid sides and arm rests, used by kings as a form of protection against treacherous or sudden attack from behind. The name was passed on to ceremonial seats of monarchs and pontiffs.

TIARA: the name of the headgear worn by the supreme pontiff, enclosed on top like a dome, topped with a cross and surrounded by three golden regal crowns known figuratively as "realms."

VERONICA: kerchief bearing the image of Christ's bloody face after, it was believed, a pious woman called Veronica (*vera-icona*, true icon) dried his holy face with the cloth, which miraculously took the impression of his features.

FOR STARTERS . . .

A glossary of curious recipes,
to whet the appetite

ABBOT'S SNAILS

✝

From an old French recipe book.

After cleaning and purging the snails well, boil them in water flavored with thyme, bay leaf, sage, rosemary and vinegar. Leaving them in their shell, transfer them to a pan with butter and diced onions. Add scalded cream. Cook over a very low flame, then thicken with egg yolks. Add salt and pepper and serve with pieces of toast fried in butter.

CARDINAL'S PEARS

✞

Take some medium-sized pears. Peel, but leave pears whole. Cook in vanilla syrup 10 minutes, then leave to cool in the liquid. Place in a dessert bowl. Pour over sweetened strawberry purée, which you have flavored with kirsch and maraschino.

COUNCIL EGGS

✠

Recipe from the Most Reverend Dominican Mothers of the Monastery of San Biagio at Lerma, Spain.

Ingredients for 6
6 eggs
a pinch of salt
4 teaspoons flour
12 slices of pork sausage
3 tablespoons oil

Separate the eggs, keeping the yolks in half of the shells. Add salt. Whisk the reserved egg whites until stiff, incorporate the flour and blend with a wooden spoon. In a frying pan, sauté sausage slices until light brown and cooked. Drain. Set aside. In the same frying pan, heat the oil until hot. Drop in a spoonful of egg white, and then place a slice of sausage on top. On top of this, put an egg yolk, another slice of sausage, then yet another spoonful of egg white.

Proceed in this fashion rapidly and with care for each egg. Arrange the eggs on a warmed serving dish, pour over a few spoonfuls of warm oil and serve immediately.

ST. PETER'S FISH (JOHN DORY), ECCLESIASTICAL STYLE

✝

A recipe with a touch of sanctity.

Ingredients per person
1 small John Dory (roughly ½ pound)
extra-virgin olive oil
half a lemon

Poach the fish in salted water for 8–10 minutes. Drain, remove the skin, fillet it and place on a serving dish. Drizzle over a little oil and sprinkle with lemon juice.

JUBILEE CHERRIES

From a French family cookbook.

Remove the pits from 2 pounds of nice red cherries. Cover with water and boil in a small saucepan with ½ cup sugar and 1 cup red currant jam for 6 to 8 minutes. Transfer to small silver bowls (fill only halfway) and take to the table. Serve after pouring over a spoonful of warmed kirsch and flambéeing!

MONSIGNOR'S POACHED EGGS

✠

Ingredients for 4

½ pound poached white fish
1 cup white sauce
4 tablespoons butter
salt and pepper to taste
8 slices French bread
8 poached eggs

Purée the fish and bind with a little of the white sauce and butter. Season with salt and pepper. Spread the purée on the bread. On top of each slice, put a poached egg, and then pour over the rest of the white sauce, diluted and thickened with butter. Bake in a fairly hot oven (400°F) for a few minutes, then serve.

PAPAL SALAMI

✝

Ingredients for 4–6
6 tablespoons butter, at room temperature
⅜ cup granulated sugar
1 egg, separated
¼ cup cocoa powder, sieved
8 hard crackers, crushed into very small pieces
3 tablespoons rum
1 tablespoon dry Marsala

Place the butter in a bowl and work together with the sugar by beating energetically with a wooden spoon. When this mixture is smooth, add the egg yolk, half of the egg white and the cocoa powder. Keep on beating and add the crackers. Blend and then flavor the resulting paste with the rum and Marsala. Use your hands to mold into a salami shape, then wrap in waxed paper or aluminum foil. Seal the ends and leave to chill in the refrigerator for a few hours. Slice and serve.

PILGRIMS' MEATBALLS

Mince 2½ cups meat left over from a roast or casserole and mix together with 1 cup mashed potato and a few tablespoons of diced onions sautéed in butter, a handful of chopped parsley, 4 eggs, salt, pepper and a sprinkle of nutmeg. Mold into meatballs, all the same size, dredge in flour and then coat with breadcrumbs. Fry in hot oil.

A WARMING PONTIFICAL SOUP

✝

A recipe from the Bassa Padana region of Italy.

Take a cup and fill it to the brim with very hot broth and *al dente* cappelletti. Pour in half a glass of sparkling red Lambrusco wine and enjoy before the holiday lunch, after High Mass (Christmas, Easter, Patron Saint). Alternative: broth and *al dente* fine tagliolini noodles.

EPISCOPAL SOUP

✠

Recipe from the Most Reverend Mothers of the Trinity, Burgos, Spain.

Ingredients for 6

2 tablespoons butter
1 tablespoon flour
4 cups good stock
4 eggs, separated
1 cup sherry
2 cups oil for frying
salt to taste

Melt the butter in a saucepan, add the flour little by little, stirring all the while. Slowly mix in the stock, stirring with a wooden spoon. In a bowl beat together the egg yolks and sherry, then pour into the stock and boil for 2 minutes. Lastly, whisk the egg whites stiff and fry small spoonfuls in very hot oil. Add to the soup just before serving. Season with salt.

ST. PETER

(A.D. 30–67)

Who pinched the pluck?

In our collective memory, the name "St. Peter" conjures up stories of distant lands, fishing in Lake Tiberias (Luke 8), the disavowal of the name of Jesus at cock-crow, tragic martyrdom in Rome, and the testimony of his faith; it also evokes ancient peasant feasts and popular religious rites followed by enormous meals.

St. Peter's feast day is always associated with food. In some agricultural areas, such as the territories south of Mantua, June 29 is harvest day for succulent pears known as "St. Peters," small fruit as yellow as honey, soft, juicy and fragrant, excellent as a snack with hearty flakes of locally produced hard cheese.

In the dog days of summer when the sun beats down, early-season melons ripen almost miraculously, their sweet smell heightened by the sultry humidity. The most prized of these melons, with a rough netted skin, are offered in the local piazzas, almost as a propitiatory rite, together with slices of garlic-flavored salami and salmon-pink ham—the color of perfect maturity—so soft that it melts in the mouth.

The origins of intensive farming of melons are lost in the mists of time. Local farm hands, who in the olden days ate melons with salt, were responsible for inventing one of the best-loved dishes of the Mediterranean diet, *prosciutto e melone*.

St. Peter, a humble fisherman from Bethsaida chosen from among the disciples to found the Church of Rome, could never have imagined that his name would become associated with piazza parties and countless dishes. He probably never remotely imagined that he, originally called Simon, son of Jonah, a man of great generosity and many doubts, would be selected by the Holy Father to lead the believers, and therefore become the first Pope.

Despite the many doubts that beset his path to sanctity, Peter's friendship with Christ was a very strong one. It was perhaps his humanity, a rather frail humanity that he overcame to achieve salvation, that has made him one of the most popular and best-loved saints among the faithful.

The Fisher Saint sustained his faith through many trials, and slowly came to realize that he was gaining great inner strength. He became fully conscious of this when, after the resurrection, Christ said to him, "Feed my sheep." Peter founded the Church and the papacy, and from that moment on, from Palestine to Syria, Asia Minor to Greece and on to Rome, where he arrived in A.D. 60, he spared no effort or courage to spread the Gospel.

It was because of this that between late June and early July of A.D. 67, Nero decided to do something to silence this elderly bearded foreigner whose passionate words could transport crowds of believers. Those included women like the famous Xanthippe, wife of an imperial high functionary who, after converting to Christianity, refused even to countenance performing her conjugal duties. The cruel prefect Albin found he had the same problem. As a result, the Apostle Peter was thrown in jail.

History tells that having received a warning, Peter made good his escape (he always did have lurking doubts!) along the Appian Way; he turned back to face his cruel fate only after Christ appeared to him, answering his question "*Quo vadis, Domine?*" ("Lord, where are you going?") with the words "I am going to Rome to be crucified again." After a spell of harsh imprisonment, Peter was then crucified, along with his wife, Petronilla. Sources agree on the date: June 29 of the year 67. Since that day, the name of Peter has been venerated not just in the Eternal City of Rome, of which he is patron saint and where he is commemorated with great feasts and solemn ceremonies, but all over the world.

His body, interred with St. Paul's outside the city walls, was rediscovered in excavations ordered by Pius XII that were begun in 1939 and completed in the 1960s. Peter now lies in the Vatican vaults along with other pontiffs.

St. Peter's tragic end and his humanity have always provided food for the imagination of Romans. Credited with many marvels, Peter was reputed to have created a spring, which still exists in the Mamertine jail, to baptize his fellow prisoners. He was also said to have a double who gave a hefty kick to anybody who approached Peter to kiss his feet without true devotion.

But the best story told of him is associated with food.

One day, the story goes, Jesus wanted to go fishing with his favorite disciples, Peter, Paul and John. At the end of a glorious day, he spit roasted a lamb, cut it into pieces and then noticed that the heart, liver and lungs—the "pluck" or *coratella*, the most prized part of the beast—were missing. He asked who had stolen them. Nobody answered, not even St. Peter, who they all knew was occasionally untruthful. Christ then handed out four of the five portions he had cut. Gluttonous Peter asked who the fifth piece was for. The Son of God answered with a smile: "It is for the man who stole the pluck." He forgave Peter and the day came to a happy conclusion.

This little anecdote, almost certainly a product of the popular imagination, is just one of many associating the saint's vocation with food.

Many cookbooks give recipes for fish bearing Peter's name. One fish in particular, as tasty as it is ugly, was classified by Linnaeus in the eighteenth century as *Zeus faber,* but is more commonly known as St. Peter's fish or John Dory. The reason for this association may lie in one of several legends. It is said that the saint found this fish caught up in his net and, seeing how ugly it was, gingerly picked it up between two fingers (marking the two black spots on its side) and threw it back in the water. Others have ventured that these marks are black because St. Peter had previously worked as a charcoal-maker; still other accounts identify them as marks of holy gratitude, since in the fish's mouth the apostle found a silver coin with which he was able to pay the excise man at Capernaum.

However many stories there may be, our fish, esteemed since ancient times for its delicate taste, crops up on tables cooked in a variety of ways.

Whether you taste it in soup, poached simply or with herbs, spare a thought for the Fisher Saint.

Let us not forget, also, that St. Peter is the patron saint of fishermen, fishmongers, harvesters—because of the time of year when his feast day falls—and also of doormen, because, it seems, God entrusted him with the keys to heaven.

✝

We dedicate the following dishes, associated with stories concocted in the popular imagination over the centuries, to the Fisher Saint.

ST. PETER'S RISOTTO WITH VIADANA MELON

✠

Created by a gifted Mantuan chef, this brand-new recipe can be eaten on the feast day of St. Peter. He's the patron saint of many cities great and small, from Rome to villages such as Viadana, in the province of Mantua.

Ingredients for 6

¼ cup olive oil
1 clove garlic, thinly sliced
1 shallot, thinly sliced
1 pound arborio rice
1 glass of white wine
1 ripe cantaloupe melon (about 2 pounds), quartered, seeded, flesh removed from rind and diced
salt
pepper
1½ cups boiling stock
1 mint sprig, chopped
1 tablespoon butter
grated Parmesan cheese for serving

In a saucepan, heat the oil and sauté the garlic and shallot until soft but not brown. Add the rice and stir with a wooden spoon. When the rice is translucent, pour in the wine and, stirring all the time, add the melon. Add salt and pepper to taste, and continue adding boiling stock, bit by bit, stirring all the time. If you need more liquid, use boiling water. When the rice is cooked, after about 20 minutes, add the mint leaf and butter to the rice. Mix well and serve hot, sprinkled with Parmesan cheese.

ST. PETER'S FISH WITH HERBS

✞

Ingredients for 6

1 tablespoon minced tarragon
1 tablespoon rosemary
1 tablespoon thyme
1 tablespoon parsley
1 tablespoon basil
1 clove garlic
pinch of ground ginger
2 tablespoons breadcrumbs
1 St. Peter's fish (John Dory) weighing roughly 3 pounds, filleted
2 eggs, beaten
all-purpose flour
oil for frying
10 tablespoons butter, melted in a frying pan
2 tablespoons dry white wine
juice of 1 lemon
salt
pepper

Combine the herbs, garlic and ginger in a mortar, crush, then add all but 2 tablespoons of the breadcrumbs. Mix well and spread over the bottom of a large oval dish. Coat the fish fillets with the egg, coat with flour and fry in the oil. When the fillets are done, drain on absorbent paper. Add herbs to the butter. Slowly add the wine and lemon juice. Blend vigorously together, until the mixture is well amalgamated. Set the golden-brown fillets of fish on the serving dish, sprinkle with the remaining breadcrumbs and serve still warm, with the piping hot sauce.

CORATELLA ALLA ROMANA

✠

Coratella, the lungs, heart and liver of the lamb, has long been a delicacy in Rome. Traditionally eaten in springtime, when the lambs are very young, the dish can be served on its own, or garnished with tender Roman-style artichokes.

Ingredients for 4

1 tablespoon lard

2 portions lamb lungs, heart and liver, trimmed, washed and cubed

1 small glass of Marsala or the juice of 1 lemon

salt and pepper to taste

In a large skillet, heat the lard over high heat until browned. Add first the lungs, then the hearts and last the livers. Cook for at least 10 minutes. Season with salt and pepper. Just before the *coratella* is done, pour in the Marsala or lemon juice. Allow to evaporate and serve hot.

This dish is extremely tasty. For a touch of extra flavor, throw at least three small artichokes, outer leaves and choke removed, per person into the pan before adding the meat.

SOLE QUO VADIS

✝

A fish dish inspired by the well-known legend of the Appian Way.

Ingredients for 4

2 tablespoons butter

4 fresh fillets of sole, lightly dipped in flour if desired

1 glass of dry white wine

a handful of whole boiled crayfish,* warm

thinly sliced white truffle, to taste

medallions of herb butter

salt and pepper to taste

In a nonstick frying pan, melt the butter until it froths. Add the sole, then pour over the wine. Cover and cook for at least 10 minutes. Place fish on a serving dish and keep warm. Boil the cooking juices until thickened and pour over the fish. Arrange the crayfish all around, then decorate with the truffle slices; top with the medallions of herb butter.

* Note: If crayfish is unavailable, substitute cooked shrimp or lobster meat.

ST. SYLVESTER I

(314–335)

Feasts and champagne for a fasting Pope

It is not easy to write about this ancient and saintly Pope, celebrated so joyously on December 31, the day of his death, with fireworks, bacchanalian New Year's Eve dinners, champagne and all-night parties. We learn from archive documents that in actual fact he was an ascetic, a faster and a hermit who was persuaded to come down from the tortuous ravines of Mount Soratte only by the despairing pleas of Emperor Constantine, who was suffering from leprosy.

It is precisely these conflicting memories of Sylvester that prompted us to find out more about how this Holy Pope fits into Christianity and the history of the Church. Jacopo da Varagine's *Golden Legend,* the most obscure of all the lives of the saints, depicts him as a sort of hero, a steadfast defender of the faith, the man who converted the Emperor to Christianity and baptized him, after his miraculous cure from leprosy, and after Constantine had fasted for a whole seven days.

Other scholars regard Sylvester as a weak man, a man of straw in the hands of Constantine, who was a brilliant statesman keen on wielding the power achieved by Christianity over pagan civilization. Constantine committed himself to overhauling the workings of the state, including its religious structures, in an attempt to lend solidity to the doctrine of the new Christian faith. At the same time, he was strengthening his own authority.

Immediately after the Edict of Milan (313), through which Constantine proclaimed equal rights for all religions, Pope Sylvester took advantage of the promised peace and began building church after church, and Rome began to take shape as a Christian city. Sylvester was responsible for the Lateran Basilica, and for churches dedicated to St. Peter, St. Lawrence, St. Agnes and St. Marcellinus. Thanks to his passion for building, he is still held to be the patron saint of bricklayers and stonemasons.

This Pope, however, became infamous in the annals of the Church thanks to a sensational forgery perpetrated by Stephen II in 753: the so-called *Donatio Constantini* (Donation of Constantine), whereby the first Christian emperor allegedly ascribed a number of territories to the Church, and acknowledged its temporal dominion over them. Only discovered to be a fake by the humanist Lorenzo Valla in the fifteenth century, this document provided the foundation of the papacy's policy for many centuries, giving rise to endless repercussions not just on Italy but on the whole of Europe.

To corroborate the authenticity of Constantine's generous yet opportunistic move, in 1248 Pope Innocent IV (1243–1254) took it upon himself to immortalize the legend on the walls of a chapel in Rome's Quattro Santi Coronati church. In actual fact, these paintings were conceived as propaganda, to emphasize the superiority of the Church's temporal power over the Empire. This explains why the sequence concludes with the picture of a pious, kneeling Constantine handing the Pope the tiara, symbolizing civil dominion over Rome, and therefore over Italy and Europe. Sylvester, the first Pope to be acknowledged by the state, had to be portrayed as equal if not superior to the Emperor. Thus, he had to be a "great man." This explains the atmospheric and imaginative legends that grew around him, frescoed in so many churches around Italy, and his association with the New Year's feasts we mentioned earlier. If we trace the inspired and fanciful truth as depicted by artists, we find out that one of these frescoes is the source of the calendar allegory of the 365 days of the year. This number was reputedly the number of steps in a dark and frightening cave inhabited by a particularly ferocious dragon; steps that the brave and saintly Pope descended, armed only with his faith and a morsel of bread, and yet succeeded in placating the beast, tying it up, and then gloriously going back up the stairs to celebrate the end of his nightmare.

The dragon symbolized paganism, and the 365 steps stood for the days of the Roman calendar, which St Sylvester is said to have brought to Christianity by baptizing Constantine. So, St. Sylvester's feast day, established on December 31 by more than just chance, alludes to the transition from the pagan era to the Christian age. It follows that every year at midnight on December 31, when in Italy revellers are replete after a huge feast of endless delicacies, traditionally including *zampone* (stuffed pig's trotters) and lentils, and intoxicated by music and high spirits, the moment we uncork the champagne, we are, without knowing it, harking back to a tale, almost a fable really, about an ancient ascetic Pope who was sanctified by popular acclaim.

No matter how long we pored over the oldest of cookbooks, it is not surprising that we found no trace of the favorite foods of a Pope who was known for fasting; at best he must have nourished himself with a few vegetables and bread. Modern-day cookbooks, at least in Italy, are full of secular and wickedly tasty dishes celebrating Sylvester, ringing in the New Year, in the hope that the future may bring many a fine thing, including (or at least) at mealtimes.

To end the year in style, and bring in the New Year as a harbinger of prosperity and plenty, there's nothing finer than a *zampone,* a gem of Po Valley cuisine, adopted the length and breadth of Italy. Felicitously garnished with lentils, a symbol and good omen of wealth and plenty, or with mashed potato or perhaps spinach leaf, when it appears, steaming on the table, it fills the hearts of all around with good cheer and optimism.

✝

This is how one grand master of Italian cuisine cooks a worthy *zampone* to perfection for a traditional Italian New Year's eve feast.

PIG'S FEET FOR THE NEW YEAR'S EVE FEAST

✞

Ingredients

pig's feet, potatoes, spinach, and lentils for garnish

Soak the pig's feet overnight, or for at least twelve hours. When you are ready to start cooking, prick the rind a number of times with a big needle or other sharp object, and make a small incision on the underside of the foot, as all experts advise. Wrap in a length of muslin, and bind tightly so that the wrapping does not open up during cooking. Using a loop of string which you have left protruding from each end, tie to the handles of a very large saucepan so that the pig's feet can be suspended in water. Cook for 6–7 hours. When it is done, the meat should be extremely soft, almost gelatinous, and yet retain its texture in the mouth. After cooking this long, the rind should be very soft too: a true gourmet wouldn't dream of not eating it together with the rest.

—Vincenzo Buonassisi, *La cucina degli italiani*

After all that, to digest the *zampone* and lentils and all the rest of it, enjoy a glass of invigorating, eupeptic Mentuccia liqueur, distilled from herbs picked in the green mountains of Abruzzo, dedicated to this saint whose name, Sylvester, derives from "silva," or wood.

MENTUCCIA DI SAN SILVESTRO

✠

A digestive liqueur made from brandy infused with a bouquet of herbs, principally mint. Emerald-green in color, it is 42° proof.

ST. GELASIUS I

(492–496)

Merci beaucoup, Your Holiness

When we plunge an eager fork into the yielding, sweet and fragrant dough of a crêpe Suzette, flambéed in bluish Luciferian Cointreau, we are oblivious to the historic events that lie behind it.

What immediately springs to mind is the Belle Époque and Suzette, one of many lovers of the Prince of Wales, the reckless son of Queen Victoria, to whose old age a Monte Carlo chef dedicated this delicious dessert. But there is so much more to be learned by turning back the hands of time far enough, through history and myth.

Let's wind back those hands to the Early Middle Ages, to A.D. 493. At the dawn of Christianity a Pope of African origins, Gelasius I, sat in Rome. On a misty early February day a large group of Rome-bound pilgrims from the far-off land of France arrived at their destination, to visit the holy sites, and to take part in the new celebrations in honor of the purification of the Virgin Mary. These were declared by this pontiff to replace the pagan, pleasure-loving "Lupercalia," in which the people of Rome, though converted to Christianity, continued to indulge with a vengeance. These pagan festivities, which ended in mid-month with the *februatio*, the purification of the city from the evil influences of demons, were attributed such strong powers in warding off plagues, looting, famines and various misfortunes that it was nigh impossible to revoke them.

Nevertheless, that is what Gelasius, valiant defender of the true faith, managed to do, persuading the Senate to abolish them. The new solemn occasion, established for February 2, was called *Candelora,* in memory of the blessing of the candles, the light of purification and the light brought in by incipient spring.

So many French pilgrims arrived in the capital of Christianity for this event that finding sufficient food for them became a problem. Pope Gelasius, a very hospitable and generous man, took it upon himself to provide them with a square meal, and arranged for a substantial distribution of milk, eggs and flour with which the pontifical cooks made *crespelle,* pancakes—the modern-day Italian name probably derives from the Latin *crispus,* curled.

Full-bellied and happy, the pilgrims prayed with great devotion, passing by in procession with their lighted candles raised, singing hymns of joy to the heavens. Grateful to the good pontiff, they returned home full of good tidings about Rome, and about that excellent food so generously offered, which they had enjoyed so much.

Pilgrims returning from Rome took Pope Gelasius I's pancakes across the Apennines and the Alps into the rolling countryside of France, where they were very well received. Indeed, they were improved upon, ennobled and bettered, served up with fruit, jam, liqueur, and with vegetables, cheese and shellfish, in the process changing their name to crêpes and becoming something of a national dish!

There is no way of knowing with certainty if this information hails from history or legend, but that should not prevent us from saying a heartfelt *merci beaucoup* to this Holy Father.

But Gelasius I went down in history—the history of the papacy—not for the legendary crêpes given to the French pilgrims, but for his unyielding battle against the paganism that still afflicted the young Church of Rome, and for a brave letter sent to Eastern Roman Emperor Anastasius I, in which, with great decisiveness, though drawing a distinction between imperial and papal authority and considering them both to be of divine origin and independent in spheres of influence, he asserted that the supreme authority was that of the pontiff, chosen by God to head the Church, and therefore society as a whole. This quasi-dogma, forcefully stated by Gelasius, had an enormous influence on the history of medieval Europe, and subsequently generated a host of misunderstandings, clashes, struggles and strife.

But there is another reason why we should remember this African pontiff: his great humanity and his love of the downtrodden and disinherited. Gelasius is acknowledged as one of the most generous and altruistic Popes ever, for having shared all his possessions, which he defined as "patrimony of the poor," with Rome's beggars and derelicts. He saved the city from famine, exhausting all his resources in the process. He did not build basilicas or grand marble monuments, but preferred to use his money and power to help anybody in need. One biographer writes, "Gelasius seemed more of a servant than a sovereign, preferring mortification and fasts to pleasures; so full of charity and generosity towards the poor was he that he himself died poor, on November 21, 1496." The St. Francis of his time!

Like so many other Popes of antiquity, Gelasius was immediately sainted by popular acclaim. We do not know how many or what miracles he performed. But as we continue to enjoy our crêpes, we can be satiated and yet mercifully and benevolently forgiven for this little, venial but delicious sin of gluttony.

✝

Perhaps the oldest recipe for making *crispellas,* the forerunner of modern-day crêpes, appears in a fourteenth-century recipe book dedicated to Charles d'Anjou:

> *Sic fa: habeas farinam albam distemperatam cum ovis, addito safrano, et pone ad coquendum in lardo tantum; et quando decocte fuerint, pone desuper zucaro vel mel. Et comede.*

> (This is how to make crêpes: obtain some white flour mixed with egg, add saffron and cook in lard; when they are cooked, cover with sugar and honey. And eat.)

CRÊPES

✝

Here is an updated recipe from the great French chef Henri-Paul Pellaprat.

Ingredients

1½ cups all-purpose flour
2 eggs
½ teaspoon salt
1 tablespoon vanilla extract
1 tablespoon sugar
1 cup cold milk
1 tablespoon melted butter
1 shot cognac or rum

Sieve the flour into a large mixing bowl. Pour in the eggs, salt, sugar and milk. Whisk together until you have a very smooth, even mixture, the consistency of thick cream. If necessary, add a little more milk, then add the melted butter and mix carefully.

The crêpe batter must be prepared at least two or three hours before use. If so desired, thin cream may be used instead of milk. In this case, omit the butter. Flavor with the liquor when the batter is finished.

To make the crêpes, heat a little butter in a round cast-iron crêpe pan the size you want your crêpes to be. Spoon in a tablespoon of crêpe batter, tilting the pan so that it spreads across the entire surface to make a round pancake. When it is brown on one side, turn over to brown the other side. Store the finished crêpes on a silver serving dish until you are ready to serve them with the sauce or finish of your choice.

Crêpes may be served *au naturel,* stuffed, rolled up or folded in four.

✞

There is no way of knowing which recipe was preferred for the Roman pilgrims, but of the many excellent recipes for this specialty, here are two to match the spirit of this book, and which are a worthy culinary homage to the memory of this generous Pope of long-gone medieval times.

CONVENT CRÊPES

✠

Prepare the crêpes as in the recipe on page 41. Stuff with sliced pears cooked in syrup, roll up and serve sprinkled with warm kirsch. We can only imagine the praises sung by the pious sisters or timorous brothers of this cheerful and hedonistic convent.

MONKS' CRÊPES

✝

Another French cookbook has a recipe for crêpes made between the austere walls of a monastery that must have been near the sea. Stuffed with a selection of seafood, these crêpes are savory and tempting.

For the batter (makes 12 savory crêpes)
1 cup plus 2 tablespoons all-purpose flour
a pinch of salt
2 eggs
1 cup milk
2 tablespoons butter, melted
2 tablespoons beer to make the batter lighter
(this small quantity of beer works like yeast)
1 teaspoon chopped tarragon
cold water

In a mixing bowl combine the ingredients, starting with the flour, then the salt, eggs, milk and butter, and then the beer, tarragon and water, until the mixture reaches a semi-liquid consistency. Leave to rest for at least an hour.

For the stuffing (for each crêpe)
1 scallop, either whole or sliced
2 medallions of meat from a lobster
8 shrimp
2 or 3 mussels
thyme
parsley
white wine

Poach all the shellfish in water aromatized with the herbs and wine, 3 minutes. Drain.

Once you have prepared the crêpes as on page 41, lay them out on the kitchen table and stuff with the shellfish, along with a sauce of your choice (American, Aurora or Hollandaise). Fold the crêpes in half, and place one next to the other in a single layer on a well-buttered baking dish which you can also present at table. Cover with the sauce of your choice and bake in a medium-hot oven (375°F) so that the sauce spreads evenly. Serve piping hot, accompanied by a good Muscadet or Rosé d'Anjou.

GREGORY THE GREAT

(590–604)

Un Papa antico che ssapeva parlà rosso e turchino
che conosceva ogni sorta de' vino
e quant'anime stanno in Purgatorio

G. Belli

(A Pope from ancient times who spoke red and deep blue
who knew every kind of wine
and how many souls are in Purgatory)

For the Pope, it is a good omen to eat cherries on April 25, St. Mark's feast day. In a ritual that has been handed down over the centuries, a nice big plate of shiny, juicy red cherries, the first of the year, always takes pride of place on the august papal table.

The misty origins of this tradition lie in the miracle of the cherries, performed by St. Mark in a dark and far-off age, a time of plague and famine, of saints and fasts. Pope Gregory I, dubbed Gregory the Great for his holiness and his miracle-working charisma, commanded with a firm hand from the pontifical throne, bulwark of Christianity against the excessive might of Byzantium and the cruelties perpetrated by the Lombards.

Nobly born, Gregory grew up in a splendid palace on the Aventine Hill. A student and devotee of the philosophy of

St. Augustine, he became a monk in humility, requesting that he be called "servant of God's servants," sleeping on a rocky floor and nourishing himself on frugal meals prepared by his pious mother based on pulse soups, a traditional Roman dish going right back to distant Latin roots. Gregory established his first monastery in a wing of his palace, and gathered together a few like-minded monks dedicated to fasting and prayer.

Later, at the behest of Pope Pelagius II, he was sent as an envoy to the sumptuous court in Byzantium, to seek alliances against the Lombard threat. A learned theologian, he had little difficulty in playing his strategic role in court politics, and he developed quite a reputation for the way he handled himself in debates.

Back in Rome, he was reluctantly appointed as Pelagius' heir. It is said that to escape this appointment he fled and hid in a wood just outside town, only for the Holy Ghost, in the guise of a white dove bathed in light, to bring the faithful to his hiding place, from which he was taken and carried triumphantly back into town. This legend has influenced traditional iconography—Gregory the Great is always depicted with a white dove close by—and the poet Giuseppe Gioacchino Belli, who in *Un Papa antico* writes,

E sti' belli segreti in concrusione
Je l'annava a ssoffià ttutti a l'orecchie
Azzeccatece chi? . . . bravi! un piccione

(So what of these great secrets?
They were whispered in his ear
By guess who . . . right! A pigeon.)

Far from being undermined by his prayers and fasting, Gregory was blessed with miraculous strength, which he used to reorganize the Church and bolster Christianity. He forced the Lombards to retreat, and persuaded Queen Theodolinda to convert, mollifying her diplomatically with magnificent gifts; he even evangelized England, entrusting the job to just fifty monks; he wrote the *Book of Rules for Pastors*, and his *Dialogues* contain many hagiographies of saints, which helped to propagate many legends. Alongside these various works, he was quick to use the patrimony of the Church in a charitable manner, distributing wheat, clothing and money to the poor.

In Gregory's day, Rome had no lack of poor. Battered and undernourished, as Paolus Diaconus writes, lashed by many natural disasters, centuries of incursions by barbarians, and food shortages, in his very first year as Pope, a flood of the Tiber destroyed the papal grain stores, and the plague decimated the population. It was during this dramatic hour that, once more, the Pope showed that his actions were guided by the Holy Ghost, who suggested he hold a propitiatory procession within the city walls. As he was praying, prostrate with the faithful by the Mole of Hadrian, the Archangel Michael appeared in a blaze of light, and unsheathed his flaming sword, signifying remission from the terrible scourge. This stunning occurrence confirmed the miracle-working abilities of the Pope, repeated on many other occasions, hence earning him the epithet "the Great."

A strange thing happened one April 25, St. Mark's day: the Holy Father, frugal by nature and by vocation, was suddenly overwhelmed—we do not know why—by an incomprehensible desire for cherries. History recounts that servants and gardeners were at a loss. The spring weather was still fresh and raw, and the cherry trees, which grew in numbers along the hills of Trastevere, from the Janiculum to the Colle del Gelsomino, were only just in blossom.

Fortunately, one gardener who was wandering the gardens in despair—gardens that, centuries earlier, had belonged to Luculus—was visited by St. Mark in a cloud of fire. The saint asked him why he was in such a state. As soon as he heard the answer, he uttered a special blessing on a tree, and in a flash it was covered in fragrant, succulent red fruit. As the story handed down through the centuries in Roman dialect recounts, the Pope "*se ne fece subito una bella panzata*" ("wasted no time in wolfing down a bellyful"). Since then, on St. Mark's feast day, the Pope usually enjoys a nice bowlful of cherries, out of not so much greed as devotion to the saint.

Although this popular legend is highly imaginative, it apparently has its origins in the ancient Roman feast of Rubigalia, founded by Numa Pompilius in honor of the goddess Rubiga, an occasion on which, as well as sampling the first cherries of the year, the Romans carried out rituals to protect crops from blight. In Christian times this holiday was transformed into Rogation Days.

✠

For such an ancient Pope, we were duty bound to pick traditional dishes from Italian cuisine, colorful and bursting with flavor, whose origins are lost in the mists of time, drawing upon ingredients typical to the Mediterranean countryside.

LEGUME SOUP

✟

This soup, mentioned by Cato, dates right back to ancient Rome. It has survived the passing of centuries and is still popular for its dietetic and nutritional properties, making it a winter favorite.

Ingredients for 6

½ cup finely chopped pork fat

1 onion, sliced

1 clove garlic, crushed

1 pound various pre-soaked beans and legumes (lentils, peas, wheat, beans, barley, etc.)

a few tomatoes (fresh or canned) or 2 teaspoons tomato paste

a pinch of cayenne pepper (optional)

In a heat-proof earthenware pot sauté the pork fat with the onion and garlic (remove the garlic from the pan as soon as it becomes golden brown). Add the beans and legumes and stir with a wooden spoon. Add the tomatoes or paste and then fill the pot with cold water. Season and simmer uncovered. The soup is ready when enough water has evaporated away. Serve warm over slices of toasted country bread. If desired, add a pinch of cayenne pepper.

CHERRIES AND PECORINO CHEESE

✞

A delicious rustic snack in honor of St. Gregory for those first warm days of April. The vital ingredients are fleshy early season cherries, still a little pink, and a mature round of Roman pecorino cheese, cut into slivers and presented in a bowl, so that everybody can pick away to their heart's content. Everybody knows that once you start with cherries, you can't stop; if you pop a little piece of good pecorino cheese into your mouth every now and then, they taste even sweeter. Tasting is believing!

OLD-FASHIONED CHERRY TART

✞

For the pastry

2¼ cups all-purpose flour
8 ounces butter, cut into small pieces
⅓ cup sugar
1 egg
grated lemon rind
salt

For the filling

2 pounds sweet dark cherries, washed and pitted
half a glass of white wine
a pinch of cinnamon
½ cup sugar
2 tablespoons breadcrumbs
3 egg yolks
1 tablespoon vanilla extract
1 tablespoon flour
1 tablespoon butter, melted
3 egg whites, whisked stiff
rosolio liqueur (page 311)

Place the cherries in a saucepan and add the wine, cinnamon and sugar. Cook 6–7 minutes until they have reduced a little and the liquid has evaporated, sprinkle over the breadcrumbs and put to one side.

For the pastry, heap the flour onto a rolling board, make a well and place inside it the butter, sugar, egg, lemon rind and salt. Knead energetically, and then leave to rest in a cool place for at least 15 minutes. Roll out the pastry into a sheet—not too thin—and line an 8-inch-diameter springform pan. Bake at 425°F for 10 minutes, remove from the oven and then fill with the cherry filling.

In a separate bowl, beat together the egg yolks and sugar and vanilla until the mixture is light and frothy, then add the flour, butter and, last of all, the egg whites. Pour this mixture over the cherries. Bake in a fairly hot oven (400°F) for 25 minutes or so. When ready, remove the pan sides and slide the tart out onto a circular dish. Leave to cool before serving, then sprinkle with rosolio liqueur.

POPE JOAN

(855–858)

Aphrodisiac cuisine for "the woman *who sat on the Fisherman's throne"**

It was food that sealed the fate of Joan, the "angelic woman Pope," whose undoing was her prolonged intake of exotic, flavorsome, spicy and, according to rumor-mongers, aphrodisiac dishes. Between love affairs and theological disputes, there could be no other end for the only woman ever to be Pope.

Very few people are aware of her mysterious story. Indeed, it is so shrouded in mystery that there are some who believe it was made up. It has been passed down to us via a number of written and pictorial sources, all dating back to just after the year 1000. These sources gave rise to a long and acrimonious debate, which subsided only in the nineteenth century, when Gioacchino Belli wrote an uncouth sonnet for her:

E quando er Papa maschio stide male
E morse, c'e' chi dice avvelenato
fu fatto Papa lei, e straportato
a San Giovanni in sedia papale.

* G. Boccaccio, *Giovanna, angelica Papessa* in *Mulieribus claris.*

> (So when the male Pope fell ill
> And died, some say by poison
> it was she who was made Pope, and carried in triumph
> to the Church of San Giovanni in the papal chair.)

In any event, the *Cronaca Universale* written by Mariano Scoto (1028–1086), a monk from Fulda, and a history recorded by another monk, Sigebert (1112), to name but the most authoritative sources, not to mention a plethora of illuminated manuscripts and prints, corroborate the existence of this mysterious woman who, following the death of Leo IV, through machinations still unknown, was elected Pope. She retained this position for just two years, five months and four days, before her life ended tragically.

It would appear that after a period of resentment and rancor in the papacy, Joan brought a respite of peace and tranquillity. Under the clever and evenhanded guidance of this extremely well-educated woman—considered a scholar for her wide-ranging theological knowledge and debating ability, not to mention her good taste, which, among other things, saw the arrival of Oriental-style spiced foods in her kitchens—this period was a felicitous interlude for the Roman Curia, which alas ended in the most dramatic manner: the Pope publicly gave birth.

Sigebert asserts that the name Joan does not feature among the official list of Popes because of the shock and shame felt by the Curia and faithful alike on witnessing her give birth to a bonny little boy slap bang in the middle of a procession. Other sources have claimed that this silence was to cover up not so much the shame of her giving birth, but the fact that a woman had reached the highest office of Christianity because of the will of the Patriarch of Byzantium, a sort of secret agent in skirts, sent by an alternative Church with designs on Rome.

Fantasy or reality? Many sources recount events in her life with too much detail for fiction, and they agree that she was stoned to death immediately after her public birth in an alleyway between San Clemente and the Coliseum, known today as Vicolo della Papessa. The woman that the faithful admired "for her elegant appearance, great learning and magnificent life"* had the misfortune to publicly reveal her sin, fulfilling the words uttered by a demon, who in the consistory shouted out to the stunned cardinals that a terrible fate awaited the future Pope.

It should be pointed out that it was the devil himself who butted his horns into Joan's eventful life, later immortalized in the Tarot deck as the High Priestess, signifying ambivalence. Born in Mainz, Germany, she ran away from home at the age of twelve disguised as a man to follow a monk, with whom she was in love, to Athens. Still in male dress, Gilberta or Agnes (which was her real name?) followed a stringent course of theological studies, after which she was far better equipped than many renowned scholars of her day; many of them were dumbfounded by the eloquence of this mysterious little seminarist, so full of divine grace and yet so elegant in her behavior and garb.

After her beloved died, the young woman turned up in Rome, where she opened what soon became a thriving

* Ibid.

school of theology. It was but a short step from here to officiating at the altar of St. Peter, famous the world over for being made from sheets of gold weighing 206 pounds each and encrusted in jewels. In those days the capital of Christianity was the destination of kings, who came to Rome for their coronations. They were much taken aback by the grandeur of the Church of San Giovanni, by the Pope's consummate hospitality, by the religious ceremonies and banquets heaped with roast meats and freshwater and sea fish, cooked with skills picked up during centuries of experience, and washed down with an extraordinary range of wines, from amber yellow to ruby red in color, served in golden goblets studded with jewels as ancient as the Eternal City itself.

Pope Joan was fully capable of fulfilling her high ministry, but even more than her predecessor, inventor of the Leonine City, she knew how to present extraordinary events at the papal court: precious vestments in fabric woven with gold and silver thread; impeccable lace-trimmed damask garments; and tables laden with exotic and Oriental foods. Sources concur that Joan was very keen on Oriental-style cuisine, had a predilection for spicy foods, considered to be aphrodisiac, for juicy fruit salads laced with honey,* and many arugula salads, whose virtues are well known. It was her passion for these foods that delivered her into the arms of a young and very handsome servant, who publicly made her a mother, to the very great shame of the Curia. And yet, after Joan, the papacy fell into the grip of notorious courtesans, such

* Galen (c. 129–200), doctor to the Emperor Marcus Aurelius, considered honey to be a potent aphrodisiac.

as the infamous Marozia (d. 955).

Whether or not Joan's amazing story is true, right up until the end of the seventeenth century, two birthing stools were set out at every conclave, continuing a ritual that began a little before the first millennium. Some scholars have claimed this symbolized the indissoluble union of the Pope with the Mother Church. The newly elected pontiff had to sit on one of these chairs and have his testicles palpated, to remove any doubts whatsoever. These high-backed porphyry chairs of ancient Roman origin, described by many historians, were housed in the Vatican Museum until Napoleon took one away to the Louvre.

Such is the fascinating story of the only woman Pope. Some have ventured that it is merely a distorted popular myth: since ancient times, in the spot where she reputedly gave birth and was stoned to death, there had stood an image of Iris with a babe in her arms; in Christian times this was replaced with a shrine to the Madonna and Child.

In any case, since this book is really about the history of food and culinary tradition, and since there are no precise references apart from the Pope's long enjoyment of aphrodisiac foods, we thought it apt to dedicate to her a number of very old recipes with an Oriental flavor, brought up to date, of course. We chose dishes based upon water game (as fish was called in those days) such as paprika oysters and aphrodisiac gilthead fish and two liqueurs, one made from honeyed onion and the other horseradish, both of which are said to have magical properties. To finish off, a luxuriant fruit salad, thickened with yogurt, as is the custom in Eastern lands.

PAPRIKA OYSTERS

✝

Ingredients for 6
30 very fresh oysters
a little butter
half a glass of dry white wine (Riesling if possible)
salt
pepper
paprika

Rinse and scrub the oysters and place in a large, shallow frying pan on a high heat. Place the butter in a small frying pan and heat until foaming. When the oysters open, extract them quickly from the shells, and then transfer to the small pan. Stir rapidly so that the shellfish do not dry out too much. Add 2 tablespoons of the oyster cooking liquor and the wine. Season to taste and remove from the heat. Return the oysters to their shells, arrange on a long serving dish, sprinkle with paprika and serve warm.

APHRODISIAC SEA BASS

Ingredients for 6
1 bottle champagne
1 teaspoon thyme
3 bay leaves
3 cloves garlic
13 white peppercorns
7 cloves
2–3 pounds sea bass
3 ounces salmon roe
13 anchovies, filleted
1 egg yolk
paprika to taste
a pinch of savory
olive oil
a generous pinch of salt
1 truffle, shaved

Prepare a potion with the champagne, herbs, spices and truffle, cover the fish with the liquid and marinate for at least 3 hours. Next, prepare a sauce using the salmon roe, anchovies, egg yolk, paprika and savory and whisk in the olive oil to thicken the mixture. Grill the sea bass, brushing delicately with the leftover potion. Serve with the sauce, if possible accompanied with aphrodisiac horseradish liqueur (page 66) or frozen vodka. Guaranteed to work!

APHRODISIAC HORSERADISH LIQUEUR

✝

Ingredients

1 tablespoon fresh grated horseradish root
6 tablespoons juniper berries
1 liter white wine

Steep the horseradish root and juniper berries in the wine for 20 days or so. Filter, pour off into a nice liqueur bottle, and drink when you are feeling down at the mouth. The same applies to the Honeyed Onion (page 67).

HONEYED ONION

✠

Ingredients
2 fresh white onions
1 liter dry white wine
½ cup honey

Use a Mezzaluna chopper to chop the onion, then steep onion in the wine, together with the honey, for 20 days or so, stirring every now and then with a wooden spoon. Filter and decant into a bottle. Leave for a few days more before drinking this excellent pick-me-up.

POPE JOAN'S FRUIT SALAD

Ingredients for 6
4 apples
3 clementines
7 dried figs
7 dates, pitted
½ cup raisins, soaked and squeezed dry
¼ cup shelled pistachios
¼ cup coarsely chopped walnuts
3 tablespoons sugar
juice of 1 lemon and 1 orange
1 tablespoon runny honey
1 small glass of kirsch
1 cup yogurt or whipped cream

Peel and cut the apples and clementines into small cubes; slice the figs and dates. Put all the fruit into a large bowl. Add the pistachios and walnuts. Sprinkle with the sugar, and bathe with the citrus juice. Lastly, mix together the honey and kirsch and add to the fruit salad. Leave to flavor for a short while. Before serving, to crown off the dish, pour over the yogurt or cream.

INNOCENT III

LOTARIO DI SEGNI

(1198–1216)

"He who touches pitch is tarred"

The fetid rooms in the ancient ruin of Septizonium were a temporary home to a handful of cardinals, in conclave for the first time. Supplied through a small opening with small portions of frugal foods in order to hasten the voting, they had the onerous task of electing a new Pope capable of guiding the tense and delicate relations between the Church and the Holy Roman Empire.

And so it came to pass that, tired, weakened and hungry after being shut up for several days, the cardinals proclaimed the new Pope. On January 8, 1198, Lotario de Segni was crowned with the tiara as Innocent III.

This election, held under new conditions, took on the character of a lay ceremony, signifying that the Church of Rome was a true State. The new pontiff was a felicitous choice, combining the mettle of a moralist (his motto was, "He who touches pitch is tarred") with deep faith and remarkable theological learning, gleaned from his many years at university in Paris and Bologna. It was no coincidence that his pontificate marked a crucial change in Italian and European history.

It has been ventured that his clearheadedness, embodied by his skillful international policies, the strengthening of trade, and the persecution of infidels during the Crusades, made the papal state strong and economically robust, a place where life and the economy were inexorably beginning to be modernized; at the same time as the economy evolved, customs, habits and tastes altered too.

In this chapter we will say less about what people ate at the Curia, or what foods the Pope particularly liked (for his part, at table he reflected the sobriety and moderation he showed in life—at lunchtime he ate just a single dish), than about the new developments of his day. The thirteenth century was marked by an opening up toward the East, including its eatables (who could forget the descriptions of what people ate in China written by Marco Polo in his book *Il Milione*), thanks to a number of happy coincidences, in which this Pope played his part.

A trade boom heralded the transition from the Dark Ages, the more strictly medieval time when the population was divided between the extremely poor and the extremely rich (nobles and clergymen). Imports of new fabrics such as silk, gems and valuables were soon followed by the first spices. Not only could the spices be used to flavor foods, they were also very useful for preserving foodstuffs (especially meats); they brought an exotic flavor to food, completely revolutionizing traditional tastes, until then limited to sweet, savory, local-grown herbs and vinegar.

At the pontiff's behest, new illustrated manuscripts compiled by herbalist doctors began to circulate, laying out new rules of hygiene. In a groundbreaking work, Pietro Massandrino wrote of the concept of "healthy eating as a way of keeping disease at bay." There was a great air of change abroad, owing mainly to a new, more open and modern concept of culture: culture as a global entity.

Two famous men were the driving force behind these changes, first as friends, then as the bitterest of enemies. In one corner, Innocent, intent on defending the Church (he launched the bloody crusade against the Albigensians that culminated in a bloodbath in 1208), while extending his borders toward the Marches and Umbria and the Matildan territories, rich in forests with wild pigs and olive trees. In the other corner, Frederick of Swabia, brought up on religious and Latin culture by the great Pope-godfather to whom his pious mother Constance of Altavilla had entrusted him at a young age. Like Innocent imbued with a great diversity of culture, but considered the Antichrist, he too was a man particularly attentive to medicine and treatment of the body, as attested to by his strengthening of the Salernitana medical school, which he transferred to Naples, and the circulation of many Arab and Jewish medical texts, including the diet recommended by Maimonides (1135–1204).

These documents, fundamental to the history of medicine and dietology in an age when cooking was more for subsistence than pleasure, and when raw materials were often extremely scarce, may be considered the precursors of modern-day cookbooks.

That is not to say that fine cuisine did not exist. It did, to the delectation of the palates of knights and ladies. Throughout the thirteenth century, in castles and later in cities, people indulged in the pleasures of life. Music, poetry, brocade braids and garments provided the setting for haute cuisine based on roast meats, especially fowl, fish pies, blancmange, and traditional wines. Meanwhile, fasters could rely on the herbs and fruits recommended by the *Regime Salernitanum.*

Pope Innocent issued drastic orders from the high ground of his castles, taking care to disempower the rival Orsini family—from whose tables, it was said, no delicacy was absent. He charitably donated food and money to the poorest people, and at the same time made sure that papal luncheons were enriched by a particular delicacy from the Hills of Jesi in the Italian Marches: barrels of Verdicchio, a wine with a slightly bitter taste, a wine to provoke a degree of euphoria, ideal for meatless days when dining on fish, or with cabbage soup, an ancient country dish whose origins are lost in the past.

The Pope served this wine to his guests in his famed tall golden goblets; it is quite possible that it was a healthy glass of Verdicchio that kept his mind so lively and his politics so lucid, and gave Frederick such a hard time keeping up with him!

The lower classes, living in severely straitened circumstances, ate what the land provided, and yet managed to bring out a great deal of flavor from very little: *farricello,* soups made of bread, turnips, beans, a little poultry, and occasionally some pork, a meat generally ignored by the noble classes because pigs ate any old rubbish.

Knights, the richest class of all in the wake of the Crusades, enjoyed the most refined foods, and it appears that they more than anyone else indulged in the pleasures of good eating during peacetime. It is said that before setting off for war they gathered around a table to celebrate an ancient rite, to which ladies were also admitted. There was something of the initiation about this elegant and refined ceremony, known as the oath of the pheasant (or peacock): a roast pheasant was brought to the table, standing erect, dressed in its own feathers, and before it all the knights uttered the same vows, in order to propitiate the outcome of the battle. With a very sharp knife, the most prominent knight then sliced the bird into a number of parts of equal size, which were eaten in a sort of lay communion—a practice commemorated several centuries later by Vincenzo Cervo in *Il Trinciante* (1581).

Though during the time of Innocent III recipe books were not yet being published, certain classical recipes had been codified, such as pheasant roasted in its feathers, or the soups eaten by the poor, dishes that, reinterpreted with new flavors, even made their appearance at opulent Renaissance feasts.

The Curia also ate in splendid opulence, if it is true that, in the early thirteenth century, radical evangelical and pauperist movements took a stand against the Church's excesses (including its gustatory ones). Innocent may have been able to silence the Albigensians, but he could not stifle the voice of St. Francis, whose new order was first acknowledged in 1209.

St. Dominic was the instigator of the most important religious event of the century, the XIIth Ecumenical Council. Chronicles report that for the event Rome played host to 70 patriarchs and archbishops, 400 bishops, and 800 abbots with their retinues. Between one debate and the next, under the pleasant Italian sun, they stuffed themselves with meat and fish, blancmange and fruit jellies, all washed down with His Holiness' finest wines.

Perhaps this helped them come to certain significant decisions, such as unification with the Eastern Church. They also compiled the *Corpus iuris canonici,* issued the Easter obligation, and laid down the fasting days (more than two hundred of them!) and the doctrine of Transubstantiation, as well as condemning usury practised by the Jews. By this time, however, he was old and tired, so worn out that not even a nice glass of Verdicchio could raise his spirits. He had fought his corner well, extremely well, and finally passed away in peace while staying in Perugia.

By a quirk of fate, the Holy Sepulchre was finally liberated a few years later, in 1228, by Innocent's former pupil Frederick, the great enemy of the Church. The Crusades were still big business.

✠

The poor subsisted on a number of highly traditional, simple and wholesome soups, such as *farricello,* cabbage soup, bread soup, and bean soup. Here is a selection.

FARRICELLO

✝

Ingredients for 6

pork rind (preferably from a ham)
1½ cups whole wheat grain
a little ham fat
1 clove garlic
1 onion
1 tablespoon parsley
a pinch of marjoram
1 tablespoon extra-virgin olive oil
1 pound peeled ripe tomatoes or canned tomatoes
salt and pepper to taste
toasted homemade bread rubbed with garlic

Wash the pork rind in cold water and boil in water to cover for 4 minutes in a small saucepan. Drain, cool and dice. Boil uncovered in a little water for an hour. Clean the wheat grain by washing it under running water in a colander with small holes.

On a wooden board, chop the ham fat with the garlic, onion, parsley and marjoram. In a large saucepan, sauté these ingredients in the olive oil until golden. Add the tomatoes and cook for 15 minutes. Add the pork rind with the water it was cooked in, and when this returns to the boil, add the wheat. Simmer for 20 minutes or so, stirring with a wooden spoon; if necessary, add a ladle or two of water. Serve when it has condensed a little, still hot, with slices of toasted homemade bread rubbed with garlic.

CABBAGE SOUP

✠

Ingredients for 6
2 tablespoons olive oil
1 onion, sliced
a pinch of pepper
1 white or red cabbage, leaves only
washed and cut into strips
a little salt
2 cups stock
homemade bread
2 cloves garlic
grated pecorino cheese to taste

Heat the oil in a heat-proof earthenware pot. Add the onion and pepper. Cook until golden. Add the cabbage. Leave to flavor for a few minutes, then add the stock. Add a little salt, if necessary, and then cook covered on a medium heat for 40 minutes. In the meantime, toast the slices of bread, rub with garlic and arrange in the soup plates. Add the hot soup and sprinkle with pecorino cheese.

BREAD SOUP WITH OIL

✝

Ingredients for 6
olive oil, preferably extra-virgin
2 cloves garlic, peeled
marjoram
1 baguette, broken into small pieces
pepper

Put the garlic, oil and a pinch of marjoram into a saucepan of water, bring to the boil, then drop in the bread. Stir continuously with a wooden spoon. When the mixture has become dense and elastic, serve in bowls, adding oil, marjoram and pepper to each helping. Serve piping hot.

PAN-ROAST PHEASANT

✝

Ingredients for 4

1 pheasant, plucked, cleaned, singed, rinsed and dried
pepper to taste
pinch of salt
5 sage leaves
6 slices bacon
3 tablespoons oil
4 tablespoons butter or chopped pork fat
2 bay leaves
1 small glass of brandy (for the modern-day version)
½ cup stock
roast new potatoes

Wash and pat dry the pheasant. Stuff the cavity with the pepper, salt and sage. Wrap well in the bacon and tie with cooking string. Brown it in a large saucepan in the oil and butter or pork fat, with more sage and the bay leaves. When it is golden brown, pour in the brandy and allow it to evaporate. Add the stock, turn down the heat and simmer for an hour or so. Just before serving, turn up the heat so that it browns. Untie before serving. Garnish with roast new potatoes.Wash it all down with a glass of Verdicchio. (If you are skilful enough to have removed the skin with the feathers intact, serve standing up covered in it feathers.

VERDICCHIO DI JESI

✟

This is an ancient wine, considered a classic, made in the Italian province of Ancona from Verdicchio and other grapes. A delicate straw-yellow in color, it is dry yet harmonious, slightly bitter, with an alcoholic strength of 11%. Ready for drinking a year after production, it makes an excellent accompaniment to seafood such as baked sea bass, fried shad or salted white bream and also goes well with soups such as cabbage soup. This wine is best served at a temperature of 37°F.

MARTIN IV

SIMON DE BRION

(1281–1285)

Eels in Vernaccia wine

In a book dedicated to pontifical "sins of gluttony" we could not fail to mention Martin IV, the gluttonous Pope *par excellence*, consigned to Dante's Purgatory, among other gluttons, because of his passion for eels in Vernaccia wine.

> . . . by fasting he purges
> the eels of Bolsena, and the Vernaccia wine.*

Besides, this French Pope, originally named Simon de Brion, whom Charles of Anjou, King of France (1206–1285) ,wanted on the papal throne at all costs, is better remembered for his appetite than for his pastoral commitment, and is generally regarded by Vatican historians as an utter disaster for the Church. So poorly was Martin IV received by the people of Rome—far from keen on a Pope imposed and dominated by a foreign sovereign—that his coronation ceremony took place in Orvieto, which, along with Montefiascone, became his residence (areas that, note, produce fine wine and excellent fish from Lake Bolsena).

All commentators of the day seem to agree with Dante, adding more and more detail of an increasingly curious and

* Dante Alighieri, *Divine Comedy: Purgatory*, canto XXIV.

intriguing nature about this incredibly gluttonous Pope. Jacopo della Lana, for example, has this to say: "He was most depraved in gluttony and other food-inspired greed, to the point that he had eels brought from Lake Bolsena which he put to drown in Vernaccia wine, then had them roasted and ate. So fond was he of this morsel that he kept wanting them brought up to drown in his room."

His room with its "Vernaccia aquarium" apart, this Pope must truly have been in possession of a special type of voraciousness, if another piece of gossip of the time is to be believed: full to bursting with those eels in Vernaccia and spices, he is reputed to have uttered: "*Bone Dei! Quanta mala patimus pro Ecclesia Dei!*" ("Good God, how much we must suffer for the Church of God!").

The fact is, his infamy as a glutton reached down through the centuries as far as Tommaseo (1802–1874), who could not resist, in his commentary on line 24 of canto XXIV of *Purgatory,* quoting a lighthearted epitaph that was said to have been chiseled into Martin IV's tomb (*super eius supulcro*): "*Guadent anguillae quod mortuus hic jacet ille qui, quasi morte reas, excoriabat eas*" ("The eels are happy because here lies dead he who, as if they were guilty of murder, had had them flayed").

According to a number of scholars, including the humanist Landino, Martin IV died of "corpulence and indigestion" because of the tasty fish from Lake Bolsena, cooked and washed down with all that Vernaccia.

It is recorded in the register of spending on food for the pontifical tables that fish accounted for 7 percent of all purchases, to be eaten, naturally, on Fridays, the day given over to penitence, but also sometimes on Saturdays and on the eve of the feast days of important saints such as St. Lawrence (August 10) and St. Anthony (November 30). Fish, principally from the rivers and lakes near Rome, arrived in the papal kitchens, particularly the eels from Bolsena, appreciated for their flavorsome white flesh. In the Middle Ages the Church sanctioned the widespread consumption of fish, as it was readily available. Eel was held in great esteem because of its fatty flesh, and was regarded as a great delicacy.*

Of course, the snakelike shape of an eel gave it the ambiguous appearance of a Lenten sin, while its image was irredeemably associated with the idea of the gluttony and guzzling of clergymen, prelates . . . and even Popes.

Many culinary texts that appeared during this century contain a variety of recipes for pies, flans and pastries featuring this savory fish, which became a symbol of irresistible gluttony and pontifical bingeing.

Returning to our greedy Pope, we know that between one eel and the next he barely managed to keep up with his high pastoral duties, influenced as he was, at all times, by the political desires of Charles of Anjou, responsible for putting him on the throne in the first place. Martin solved his problems by handing out excommunications left, right and center when he felt that his authority, or that of his sponsor, was

* Centuries later, Erasmus of Rotterdam (1466–1533) was appalled at the idea that a high prelate or nobleman could be admitted to heaven simply for being observant of abstinence from meat while wolfing down the best-regarded fish (including eel) when, on the contrary, a poor man would be dispatched straight to hell for chewing his way through a two-penny plate of beans and pork rind.

under threat. He even excommunicated all the Sicilians who, in the so-called Sicilian Vespers uprising of 1282, rebelled against the excessive power of the Angevins, and offered the island on a silver dish to be made a protectorate of the Holy Father.

Martin IV died of indigestion in Perugia on March 28, 1285. In accordance with an ancient and strict custom, his body was washed in heated Vernaccia, spiced with a secret blend of special herbs supplied by the pontifical pharmacist.

EELS IN VERNACCIA À LA MARTIN IV

✠

This recipe would seem to be the one that Dante Alighieri cites in his famous Canto from the *Purgatory*.

Ingredients for 6

around 1½ pounds eels
¾ cup Vernaccia wine or dry white wine
3 cloves garlic
1 onion, sliced
oil and butter for frying
1½ cups stock
pinch of salt
pepper
1 tablespoon flour

Clean and skin the eels, cut them into chunks and leave them to marinate in the Vernaccia. Fry the garlic and onions; add the eels, a few spoonfuls of marinade and stock as required. Once the fish is cooked, adjust the seasoning and serve the chunks of eel in a warmed dish, covered in the Vernaccia cooking sauce thickened with a little flour.

Eat and remember him, the greediest of all Popes.

EEL PIE

✝

Take the eels, boil 10 minutes or until half done. Add parsley, mint and marjoram. Leave to cool and fillet by hand. Discard skin and bones. Carve out small medallions, clean with boiled water, then beat medallions a little with a meat pounder. Take a pound of ground almonds, and cook until thickened, then leave to cool with giuncada* cheese. Then put all these things into a pie dish, make a crust with mixed herbs inside, and cover with strong spices, saffron and twelve minced dates. Remove when cooked. Add olive oil to moisten.

—Guerrini Olindo

* A fresh cheese drained in a basket made of entwined rushes.

VERNACCIA

✞

The origin of this wine's name is still a source of debate. Some scholars claim that it comes from the Latin *verna,* meaning household servant, and the adjective *vernacea,* which would mean "wine for the servants." We have seen for ourselves how highly appreciated this wine was by the courtly and refined pontifical palate.

Made from Vernaccia grapes, it is light and golden in color, with a delicate yet penetrating aroma. It has a dry, harmonious taste with a hint of bitterness. It is also available in sweet and reserve versions, and is made according to an age-old technique. This was the first Italian wine to receive a DOC denomination, in 1966. Excellent as an aperitif, it goes well with white meats but comes into its own, served well chilled, with all types of fish—not just papal eels.

It is produced mainly in Tuscany, but is also made in Lazio and Sardinia.

BONIFACE VIII

BENEDETTO CAETANI

(1294–1303)

Gilded forks and spoons for the Pope who called the first Jubilee

If we could journey in our mind's eye to sit at the table of this great and controversial pontiff, we immediately would be dazzled by the sparkle of gold, silver and silk. Surrounded by luxury and wealth fit for a real king, it is like being in the presence of an immense and undisputed power, an impression manifested even in the apparently minor details of everyday life. Archives filled with richly detailed inventories are the guide to our curiosity in reconstructing Boniface's character through the less well known facts of his life; but no less intriguing and significant for that.

Thus we know that on his table, Boniface VIII (born into a noble and wealthy family from Anagni) had solid-gold spoons and *furcelle* (forks with three tines, a real rarity at that time), and solid gold saltcellars and sauceboats; cups and glasses gleamed with the transparency of semiprecious stones. Everything sparkled on tablecloths of white or pink Parisian linen, or on shiny silk from Lucca—a revealing insight into this sovereign Pope, educated and trained during his studies in Todi and Bologna, and through his ecclesiastical relations with France and England.

Boniface acceded to the papal throne after "strongly advising" the weak and modest Celestine V to resign, and then presented himself as the consolidated and unrivaled expression of religious authority over all other claimants to power, including the emperor. In other words, the papacy was to take the form of an absolute monarchy; this was the byword of his domestic and foreign policies.*

As was his custom throughout his life, Boniface's table had to be of the utmost splendor. Kings, ambassadors and cardinals sat near him, but not actually at his table, which was placed higher than theirs so that all were aware of their position: everyone knew right away with whom they were dealing.

Not just the fixtures and fittings, but the foods must have shared the same qualities of rarity, abundance and refinement. A swarm of highly trained professionals—head chefs, soup specialists, breadmakers, cellarmen and spice experts—thronged the *coquina dominica,* the Pope's kitchen, also known as the "secret kitchen." These employees bore enormous responsibilities: on their shoulders rested not just the gastronomic prestige of His Holiness' table, but that of his safety.

Indeed, Boniface VIII lived in terror of poison. Such was his fear that poison had been secreted into some tasty morsel that he required his cellarmen to stand before him *(coram domino)* while he was being poured water or wine. Before he was presented with his dish, he gave his head chefs the *assazum,* a utensil for tasting foods in order to prove that they

* Celestine V, Pietro da Morrone, hermit, founded the congregation of the Celestines. Elected Pope in 1294 for his great holiness, he was disappointed by the worldly pleasures of the Curia, and abdicated after five months, opening the way for B. Caetani, the future Boniface VIII.

were not poisoned. We know from the inventory of papal treasure that Boniface had a huge collection of these instruments, of all sizes: shaped like a unicorn, said to be ideal for revealing the presence of poisons, fashioned like a sapling or in the form of a snake's forked tongue. His collection was rounded off with an infinite number of "magic knives" that were said to reveal poison when used to cut food. All of this betrayed Boniface's great fear, nay terror, of being surrounded by treacherous people in the pay of his enemies. But what enemies could the Holy Father have? Surprisingly—or perhaps not so surprisingly after all—Boniface had no shortage of foes. To start with, his questionable election, and the enforced disappearance of the pious Celestine V, brought upon him the ruinous wrath of the Colonna family cardinals, supporters of the hermit Pope, who accused him of simony and even of sodomy!

Then there was Philip IV of France, who confiscated all ecclesiastical property within his country, and thundered against the interference of this pontiff in his kingdom, which was rapidly becoming a strong and united nation-state.

Once he allowed himself to rest easy about the dangers of poisoning, the Pope at last began to settle down to banqueting, enjoying the delicacies put before him by his skillful cooks. The pontifical court register of expenses reveals that beef, pork, kid and lamb, not to mention game of the feathered and furred kind, and river and sea fish, appeared on the papal table in a thousand guises. Meat was eaten as many as four times a week; fish replaced it on fasting days. Vegetables arrived depending on the season, fresh from the surrounding countryside and Roman market gardens. The Pope's bread, made with special flour known as *somolela*, was cooked twice a week; sugar and valuable spices such as pepper, saffron and cinnamon were purchased in bulk, although these were sometimes given as gifts to His Holiness by ambassadors and foreign sovereigns.

The register of expenses shows that the Pope and his court enjoyed a very varied, balanced and, for the time, almost nutritionally perfect diet, rounded off with plenty of wine, which among other things was esteemed for its nutritional value. The Pope's favorite wine was Cesanese del Piglio, a red from the hills near his beloved hometown of Anagni, a wine of ancient nobility said to have descended from the vineyards of the Emperor Nerva.

Suspicious of Roman water fountains, and a sufferer from kidney stones, Boniface VIII had water brought in by the barrelful from the nearby springs at Fiuggi, renowned since ancient times for their therapeutic purity. This most informative register of expenses provides detail on exactly how it was transported and exactly what it cost.

When it comes to painting a picture of this Pope at table, it seems apt to picture him against the solemn backdrop of an Easter lunch, when, following an age-old custom, he sat down with the cardinals to eat a roast lamb that he had blessed. The scenario for this holy gastronomic representation required an accurate reconstruction of the Last Supper, with a clean white tablecloth on a long rectangular table; the Pope sat in Christ's place, the Prior of the Basilica (Santa Maria Maggiore) sat in Judas' spot, while the other apostles, represented by cardinals and deacons, reclined in classical style. After eating the roast lamb, probably garnished with fresh spring vegetables and washed down with the ever-present Piglio red wine, the august assembly was edified with songs and celestial chants performed by cantors brought in specially for the occasion.

This symbolic reconstruction, with Boniface in the role of Christ, seems to foreshadow the major observance that he initiated and orchestrated. Indeed, it was this Pope who accommodated the swell of penitence, expiation and conversion that was sweeping across Europe during those years. Pilgrimages, indulgences and the Crusades had helped to whip up a climate of expectation, which he focused into the idea of a Jubilee, held one year in every hundred, for general *perdonanza*, prayer and redemption, a way of renewing the world from that moment onward. This potent idea rose up from the people, rather than being handed down from the ecclesiastical hierarchy, but Boniface's personal interest turned it into an epoch-making reality, the pride of his pontificate.

On February 22, 1300, at San Giovanni, in a stentorian and dramatic voice, Boniface VIII* declared that the time of general *perdonanza* was open for all who, during that year, visited the basilicas of St. Peter and St. Paul. Pontifical messengers distributed throughout the Catholic world the Bull, which ended in these lines to aid people's memory:

Annus centenus—Romae semper est Jubileus
Crimina laxantur—curi poenitet ista donantur
Hoc declaravit—Bonifacius et roboravit.

(Every hundredth year in Rome is always a Jubilee year

* See the Giotto fresco at San Giovanni in Laterano.

Sins are absolved, punishments amnestied
So said and confirmed by Boniface.)

As these verses were being engraved on church walls along the roads leading to Rome (they are still visible on a few modest houses in the Apennines around Parma, and on the architrave of the main entrance to Siena Cathedral), parish priests and preachers recited them; pilgrims walking toward the capital of Christendom sang them out at the top of their voices, beating time with their pilgrims' staffs.

But the Pope's detractors, who immediately saw the Jubilee as not much more than a huge fund-raising exercise for the spendthrift Treasury of the Curia, immediately altered the words, replacing *laxantur* (are absolved) with *taxantur* (are taxed) . . . the Jubilee as a "tax on sins"!

An enormous number of fervent pilgrims descended on Rome. The city was invaded by hundreds of thousands of worshipers, who left their homes across Italy, and indeed Europe, to cleanse themselves of sin at the true source of salvation, braving dangers and discomforts of all descriptions along the roads they traveled, many of which were infested with brigands and bandits. The Jubilee did raise a huge amount of money in generous offerings that the pilgrims left at holy sites, but above all it rekindled in Boniface the idea of his absolute primacy among the sovereigns on earth. "At that time Boniface could taste in its fullness the feeling of his almost divine power" (Gregorovius).

But this triumph was not enough to silence his denigrators, such as Jacopone da Todi (who was thrown in prison for his views). Jacopone continued to describe him as:

Lucifero novello
a sedere en papato
lengua de blasfemia
ch'el mondo hai venenato.

(A brand new Lucifer
In the papal seat
A blasphemer's tongue
That has poisoned the world.)

As for Dante Alighieri, he couldn't put him in the *Inferno,* because Boniface was still alive, but he let him know that there was a place waiting for him among the horde of simoniacs: Dante noted, "*il mal prete a cui mal prenda*" ("May evil take the evil priest").

Neither the detested Colonna family nor Philip IV allowed themselves to be blinded by this public triumph. On the contrary, the King of France continued to spread his "libellous pamphlets" against this Pope, accusing him of being an impostor. Totally oblivious to the hail of excommunications that rained down on him from Rome, Philip planned a punitive expedition against Boniface.

At this point history takes on the hue of legend, and legend is tinged with tragedy: this pontiff who had started so enthusiastically ended up abandoned by all in his ancestral dwelling, a beaten man.

To the cry of "Death to Boniface and long live the King of France," on September 7, 1303, the banner of Philip IV, embellished with the golden fleur-de-lis of the Capetian arms, swept into Anagni. Seeing the blackness of the situation, Boniface put on his holy vestments and said: "*Da che per tradimento, come Cristo, voglio essere preso e morire come Papa*" ("Because I have been betrayed, I want to be captured like Christ, and die as a Pope"). But instead of dying a holy death, he was merely slapped in the face! Whether the slap meted out with scorn by the iron-gloved hand of Guillaume de Nogaret (emissary of the French, but in league with the Roman Sciarra family, a branch of the unpopular house of Colonna) was actual or metaphorical matters little, as this gesture signaled the collapse of an authority whose time had come.

This great, ambitious and authoritarian Pope, who had done more than any of his predecessors to immortalize himself in an enormous number of monuments (some of which still stand in Florence, Orvieto, Bologna and at the Lateran Basilica) "was the last to conceive the idea of the hierarchical Church dominating the world" (Gregorovius).

With Boniface apparently closer to the earth than to heaven, this spelled the end of an era. The papacy moved off to Avignon, beginning a long and troubled period for the Church.

Boniface VIII died in Rome, not long after that slap in Anagni, on October 7, 1303, physically and mentally broken, "a mere shadow of the great Pope he had flattered himself he was."*

He was buried in St. Peter's.

* C. Rendina, *I Papi, storia e segreti* (Rome, 1996).

✞

Gesù (sulla croce) . . . come va? . . . Gesù come va, Gesù non mi riconosci? Sono Bonifacio . . . Bonifacio, il Papa . . . come chi è il Papa! Andiamo . . . è il pastore, quello che viene da Pietro con tutti gli altri in fila . . . non mi riconosci? . . .

—Dario Fo, *Il mistero buffo*

(Jesus [on the cross] . . . how's it going? . . . Jesus, how's it going? Don't you know who I am, Jesus? I'm Boniface . . . Boniface, the Pope . . . What do you mean, "What's a Pope?" Come off it . . . he's the shepherd, one of a long line from Peter right down . . . don't you know who I am?)

TIMBALE À LA BONIFACE VIII

✝

In an old gastronomical guide we came across a recipe from the little town of Anagni, which cites our Pope's name. It is a rich and heavy pasta dish, very nutritious and elaborate, perfect for an important pontifical (or similar) banquet.

For the pastry (ingredients for 4)
1⅔ cups all-purpose flour
4 tablespoons softened butter
2 eggs
a pinch of salt
¼ cup ice water

Make the pastry roll and line a timbale (casserole) mold, which you have buttered and sprinkled with flour. Remember to leave a little pastry dough for the top, which you will roll out and cook separately on a lightly buttered baking tray. Once the pie crust is cooked, allow to cool, remove from the mold and keep to one side, together with the lid.

For the filling
1 pound egg fettuccine
2 cups prepared meat sauce

8 ounces chicken livers, sautéed in oil and butter and flavored with parsley and mint

10 ounces porcini or wild mushrooms, sliced thinly and cooked in oil and herbs

½ black truffle, sliced wafer thin

2 slices ham

Cook the fettuccine in plenty of lightly salted water, drain and place in a mixing bowl. Mix in with the meat sauce. Begin to fill the pie crust, which you have returned to its buttered mold, alternating layers of pasta, chicken livers, mushrooms, truffle and ham. Finish up with a slice of ham. Cover with the pastry lid, then bake for 10–15 minutes so that it warms through. Remove the timbale from the oven. Allow to sit for a couple of minutes, turn out into a round dish and serve.

This is a recipe worthy of a Pope's appetite.

ROAST LAMB IN THE STYLE OF POPE CAETANI

✠

Otherwise known as Roast Lamb Roman Style.

Ingredients for 4

1 leg of lamb weighing roughly 2 pounds
1 slice pork fat, finely chopped
1 clove garlic, finely chopped
1 sprig fresh rosemary, finely chopped
a pinch of salt
2 tablespoons olive oil
freshly ground pepper
1 glass of red wine

Make incisions in the leg of lamb, mix the pork fat, garlic and rosemary and stuff the mixture into them. Season with salt and pepper. Place the meat on a baking tray with quite high sides, rub the oil on the meat and cook in a medium-hot oven (375°F) for 30 minutes or so. When it is brown on top, baste with the red wine and continue cooking at the same heat for another 15 minutes, until it is done.

Serve garnished with roast new potatoes or a nicely dressed fresh leaf salad, and to pay homage to the Holy Father, accompany with a nice bottle of Cesanese del Piglio red wine.

CESANESE DEL PIGLIO

✠

Boniface VIII's favorite wine is one of the few reds produced in Lazio, specifically in the hills of the province of Frosinone, around the towns of Pugli, Anagni, Paliani, Acuti and Serrone.

Ruby red in color, bordering on burgundy red when aged, it has a winy and delicate aroma with a bouquet of violets. Soft, dry and ever so slightly bitter in the mouth. 12% alcohol. Aged in oak barrels for at least a year, it keeps well for over five years. Served at a temperature of between 65° and 68°F, it goes very well with pasta and meat dishes, roasts in particular.

CLEMENT VI

PIERRE ROGER

(1342–1352)

Sur le pont d'Avignon on y mange . . . on y boit

The history of one of France's great wines is indelibly linked with our accounts of papal gourmandizing. It is a powerful, full-blooded wine, with a high alcohol content, as red as blood, rich in flavors and aromas, dense and mellow, ideal for sumptuous medieval banquets when an entire wild boar or a quarter of beef was brought, crispy and dripping with fat, from the spit in one of the huge, smoke-filled palace kitchens, to triumph on the table of princes or high prelates.

The wine in question is Châteauneuf-du-Pape, perhaps the noblest of all French wines, which flowed freely into the gold and silver goblets of the Popes and cardinals who betrayed Rome for Avignon. In a valley blessed with plenty of sunshine and highly fertile soil, the small town near Avignon that for centuries has produced this magnificent beverage, once the pride of pontifical banquets, today a glory of French oenology, took its name from the Popes who used to spend their summers in the local castle, long since reduced to a pile of stones.

The Pope most closely associated with this divine nectar was Clement VI, Pierre Roger, elected on May 7, 1342, forty years or so after the highest pontifical authority had moved to the powerful towers of the Avignon palace. French through and through, Clement VI never thought to return to Rome. On the contrary, he purchased Avignon for 80,000 florins from Queen Joan I of Naples, whose domain it was, to make it all his own. Rome was a long way away, and Clement had entrusted the Italian city to the young Cola di Rienzo (1313–1354), a notary of the Roman civic treasury, who with his banquets and passionate speeches on the Republican ideals of peace and liberty from the Capitoline Hill had, for the time being, captured the hearts of his fellow citizens.

And so it transpired that ancient Avennio, initially a Roman colony of Narbonne Gaul, a little medieval village looking down from between the bends of the River Rhône, became a second Rome, with the whole Curia working at full tilt; Avignon soon became the beating heart of a new empire that had very little to do with spirituality.

Indeed, during the time of Clement VI, Avignon became Europe's most flourishing center of trade, and, after Paris, the most important city in France. Everything could be bought here, from the rarest spices to weapons. Tuscan merchants sold prized Lucca silks to cardinals and courtesans, hawked helmets, swords and armor to mercenary captains, and bought goods that, following the course of the Rhône, made their way down from Flanders and England.

Thousands of people lived on the fringes of the opulent papal court, which provided business for more than fifty currency exchange shops. As many as a hundred hotels and inns catered to the hordes of adventurers, whores, merchants, alchemists and traders, not to mention Florentine and Sienese bankers, ready to mop up the rivulets of gold that trickled down from the sale of indulgences, prebends and the more or less licit wheeling and dealing in which even some high prelates dabbled. Shocked by all this moral degradation, Petrarch dubbed Avignon "Babylon."

> *. . . de l'empia Babilonia ond' è fuggita*
> *ogni vergogna, on'ogni bene è fori*
> *albergo di dolori, madre d'errori*
> *son fuggito io per allungar la vita*
> —F. Petrarch, *Rime*, C. XIV, 1–4

> (From impious Babylon whence
> All shame has fled, where all goodness is gone
> And suffering has taken its place, mother of all wrong,
> I fled to save my life.)

Clement VI, who had a particular penchant for the salon life, according to one biographer suffered from "lavish megalomania," and, we may add, hedonism. He enlarged his palace and had it furnished with great pomp, drawing upon the most refined taste of the greatest Italian artists and craftsmen of the day. He wore damask and ermine (68 pelts for a cap, 430 for a cape, and 310 for a mantle). As a lover of luxury, eating habits included, he had all his tableware wrought out of solid gold (431 pounds of gold) and decorated with his coat of arms, to be set, glinting, on precious Flanders linen or Italian silk tablecloths.

At his meals, invitations for which were much sought after by illustrious guests, everybody ate with their hands, kings included, as a precaution against animated conversations degenerating into duels or attacks. Only the Holy Father was allowed to use a knife. August dinner guests were to be seen seizing succulent pieces of roast meat, and washing them down with the Pope's favorite prestigious wine.

The rich menus of this epicurean Pope also featured delicious soups, cheeses and many, many pies (for his coronation, 50,000 pies were baked, using 3,250 eggs!) stuffed with meat, fish and vegetables, followed by rich desserts of honey and spice. Banquets consisted of as many as thirty separate courses, with pauses for performances by acrobats and jesters, as well as games and (always valuable) surprise gifts, plus concerts and dances before the eagerly awaited final dessert.

Avignon was a real "party town." This Pope, whose motto was never to let any of his guests leave his noble presence disappointed, applied this to the letter when a delegation of Roman citizens, led by Cola di Rienzo, knocked on his door to request a new Jubilee Holy Year, after just fifty years rather than the hundred decreed by Boniface VIII.

Petrarch too added his own poetic comment:

Quis ad extremae longissima tempora vitae
prevenit, aut aevi cenenos conficit annos?

(Who, at the bitter end of an extremely long life,
ever reaches the age of a hundred?)

St. Bridget* of Sweden also sent the Pope a petition, beseeching him to turn over a new leaf. In her letter, read by the Pope

* St. Bridget, a Swedish princess born around 1303, founder of the Brigittine Order, like St. Catherine of Siena urged the Popes of Avignon to return to Rome.

with great respect and solemnity, she entreated him to unite Christian pilgrims in Rome for a new moment of redemption. Besieged by so many heartfelt voices, Clement VI made a few quick calculations and concluded that by reviving the ancient Hebrew custom of a Jubilee every fifty years he could satisfy the Romans, maintain his prestige from a distance, and give a huge fillip to the finances of his rather costly "Babylon."

Insincerely borrowing a phrase from St. Paul to exalt the spirit of the Roman people, and allowing them to hope that he might in the future return to Rome, he declared: "*Desidero enim videre vos*" ("I wish to see you") and proclaimed a Holy Year Jubilee for 1350.

Despite the great plague of 1348 (described by Boccaccio in his *Decameron*) and an earthquake that seriously damaged Rome, and of course the absence of the Pope, who was extremely wary about leaving the land of plenty at Avignon, the 1350 Jubilee was one of the most devout and sincere of all time.

Multitudes of pious pilgrims flocked to Rome from throughout Europe to pray in the basilicas and the sites appointed for penitence and worship, and make their offerings, as they said, to "earn" indulgences. They braved the thousand perils and obstacles of the Francigean Way, the ancient road more than 1,000 miles long linking northern Europe (starting in Canterbury) to Rome, for centuries the backbone of trade and traffic, and converted into the path of faith and salvation. The most traveled route went over the St. Bernard Pass, then down across the pleasantly green Po Valley plain before crossing the Apennines. A stopover at

Altopascio, the biggest reception center along the whole route, and then onward to Poggibonsi and Siena, where the road merged with the Via Cassia, the historic Roman road running through the Val d'Orcia, before climbing steeply on past Radicofani, and then, at last for the exhausted pilgrims their destination, *Caput Mundi.*

The Holy Year briefly restored Rome as the capital of Christianity. It also provided an opportunity for many unscrupulous people to enrich themselves: "butchers mixing and selling with subtle deception bad meat with good," bakers charging a fortune for bread, and hoteliers speculating on the tiredness of pilgrims selling six or seven of them a single bed, according to G. Villani in his *Cronache.*

A Roman rhyme has preserved the memory of these occasionally bawdy promiscuities brought about by the invasion of foreigners:

Pellegrino che vienghi a Roma
rotte le scarpe porti a li pie'
oilà, oilè
Io ne vengo da la Francia
e so'n povero pellegrì
oilà, oilè
Anderemo dal signor oste,
se vole alloggia 'sto forestie'
oilà, oilè . . .
Io la tengo 'na camera sola
dove riposa la mia moglie'
oilà, oilè

Quando fu la mezzanotte
lo forestiero che s'alza in pie'
oilà, oilè
Forestiero porcaccio fottuto
te sei fottuto la mia moglie'!
oilà, oilè . . .

(Pilgrim who comes to Rome
wearing worn-out shoes on your feet
oilà, oilè
I come from France
And I'm a poor pilgrim
oilà, oilè
We'll go to the innkeeper
Who'll give this foreigner lodging
oilà, oilè . . .
I've only got one room
Where my wife is resting
oilà, oilè
At midnight
The foreigner gets up and leaves
oilà, oilè
Dirty bloody foreigner
You screwed my wife!
oilà, oilè . . .)

From afar, delighting in all those newfound lost sheep, Clement counted the sparkling gold coins of alms that his emissaries sent up from Rome. "From the offerings made by pilgrims great treasure accrued to the Church, and the Romans, by selling their goods, all became rich" (G. Villani, *Cronache*).

As we began by talking about wine, it is only suitable to conclude this tale with another wine that also made its appearance on the table of this august pontiff. Francesco di Marco Datini, a merchant from Prato in Tuscany, was one of those who during the time of Clement VI set up in the main square in Avignon, shuttling back and forth to import the light and flavorful Chianti wines from his homeland, and even sell them at a premium after persuading the French to drink plenty before tucking into the Châteauneuf-du-Pape.

"Bringing wine to Avignon from Italy, the merchant from Prato had, in a certain sense, laid preparations for the return of the pontiff to Rome. As strange and irreverent as this may seem, everything is possible when, as in this case, wine and history join forces."*

Clement VI, who most certainly enjoyed Datini's Chianti, died in Avignon on December 6, 1352, and was buried at the Chaise Dieu Abbey in the Upper Loire.

* P. Accolti, *Vini di Francia.*

AVIGNON-STYLE CREAM OF CHICKEN SOUP

✠

It is often the case that good recipes travel with the gourmets who prize them. This is true of a soup that the Tarlatis, bishops from Arezzo, for obvious reasons frequent travelers to Avignon, brought to the attention of the refined pontifical tastebuds. Hearty yet delicate, in Arezzo it was known simply as "chicken soup." This soup came back to Italy in a revised form, softened and flavored by chefs from the papal court, with the high-flown name "Avignon-style cream of chicken soup," though in France it began, and to this day remains, "crème de volaille."

Here is the recipe, hot from the kitchens of the Avignon pontiffs.

Ingredients for 6

1 small chicken weighing roughly 3 pounds
ingredients for stock (onion, carrot and celery, salt, pepper, a pinch of cinnamon)
4 cups buttery white sauce
1 small clove garlic, chopped
butter
olive oil
nutmeg
cheese for sprinkling

Boil the chicken in water with the ingredients for the stock plus salt (for a stronger flavor, stud the onion with cloves and then enclose in muslin) until it is well cooked and the meat begins to come away from the bones. Remove all the meat and chop, then remove the celery and carrot and chop. Sieve the chicken broth well and reserve. Put butter and a drop of oil in a pan with the celery, carrot and garlic and flavor the meat. Blend the white sauce with the chicken broth, and add to this cream the flavored chicken meat, bring to the boil, check the seasoning, and then flavor with a pinch of nutmeg. Allow the cream to thicken and serve piping hot with a little cheese sprinkled on top, and slices of toast.

In true French fashion, for elegant luncheons you can follow this with sponge cake and mini-profiteroles.

LEYVRES EN ROST

(SPIT-ROAST HARE)

✠

A fourteenth-century French cookbook contains a recipe that seems a perfect accompaniment to the potent papal red wine. This successful union of game,* fire and wine would seem to embody the ideal of gastronomy at the time.

> *Sans lever, lardez et le mengez à la cameline ou au saupiquet, c'est assavoir en la gresse qui enchiet en la lechefricte, et y mettez des ongnons menuz couppez, du vin et du verjus et ung pou de vinaigre et e gectez sur le lièvre quant il sera rosti, ou mettez par escuelle.*

> (Without washing it, lard and eat it with cameline† sauce or with hot sauce, that is to say with the fat that runs into the dripping-pan, and put in onions chopped finely and

* Since ancient times, hare has not just been prized for its delicious taste, but has also been associated with certain powers, including that of making whoever eats it beautiful for seven days. It used to be believed that the blood of a hare would bring thick hair to the heads of the bald, and could be used to heal cuts. Lastly, a hare's leg hidden beneath the pillow of an adulterous wife was said to make her reveal her infidelity and the name of her partner during sleep.

† "A genus of cruciferous plants; spec. the 'Gold of pleasure' (*Camelina sativa*)" (OED).

verjuice* and a little vinegar. Pour over the hare when it is roasted, or put into bowls.)

This is a translation of the original recipe from the 1300s. Now let's look at a modern-day version.

Ingredients for 6
1 young hare
1 small slice pork fat
1 onion
½ cup red wine (Châteauneuf-du-Pape!)
juice of 1 lemon mixed with a little water
1 tablespoon wine vinegar
salt

Carefully skin the hare, removing also the membrane that covers the meat. Cut away the sinewy parts as well. Rub with small pieces of pork fat. Run through with a spit, and place on a grill above a dripping-pan. Cook for half an hour or so over a very high heat, or in a hot wood-fired oven, basting the hare frequently in its own juices. The meat must be tender, juicy and pink. Slice the onion and cook in the dripping juices with the wine, lemon juice and vinegar for 5 minutes, until it thickens, while carving the hare. Serve both sauce and hare piping hot, and season at the last moment.

It goes without saying, the ideal wine to accompany this dish is Châteauneuf-du-Pape!

* The sour juice of unripe grapes used as a condiment.

CHÂTEAUNEUF-DU-PAPE

✠

> A robust wine for robust and virile meals. Weak men, spinsters prone to fainting fits, finicky persons who eat rice and butter and boiled vegetables are advised not to attempt this trial, which is reserved for lovers of rich dishes, game, strong meats, spicy sauces, the aroma of garlic and fermented cheeses.
>
> —P. Accolti, *Vini di Francia*

This wine has an intense cardinal-purple color (so say the French!), a vigorous yet delicate flavor, and a pleasant tannic aftertaste. A wine with a high alcoholic content (12–14%), which is matured for a long time, it requires at least 3 years' aging to reach a level of quality that is no longer susceptible to distortion. Suitable for roast meats, rare steaks, game and fermented cheeses such as Camembert. A white Châteauneuf-du-Pape is also produced, but it is extremely rare.

HONEY-CANDIED ORANGE PEEL

✞

As a final *dulcis in fundo,* here is a real delicacy that most certainly would not have been lacking at the end of one of those sumptuous Avignon banquets: peel from an orange, a rare and expensive fruit, candied with honey and spices, the very height of fourteenth-century refinement.

This is how the recipe has been handed down to us, courtesy of an old French version:

Pour faire Orengat:

Mettez en cinq quartiers les pelures d'une orange et raclez à un coustel la mousse qui est dedans, puis les mettez tremper en bonne eaue doulce par neuf jours et changez l'eaue chascun jour: puis les boulez en eaue doulce un seule onde, et ce fait, les faictes estendre sur un nappe et les laissiez essuier très bien, puis les mettez en un pot et du miel tant qu'ils soient tous couverts, et faites boulir à petit feu et escumer, et quant vous croiez que le miel soit cuit (por essaier s'il est cuit, ayez de l'eaue en une escuelle, et faites dégouter en icelle eaue une goutte d'icelluy miel, et s'il s'espant, il n'est pas cuit: et se icelle goutte de miel se tient dans l'eaue sans espandre, il est cuit) et lors devez traire vos pelures d'orenge, et d'icelles faites par ordre un lit et gettez poudre de gingembre dessus, puis un autre, et getter usque ad infinitum; et laisser un mois ou plus puis mengier.

This is how we might make this age-old delicacy nowadays.

Ingredients

2 organic oranges with good thick peel
2 cups honey
ground ginger

Remove the peel from the oranges, scrape out and discard the pith, and cut into thin strips. Soak in fresh water for 7 days, changing the water every day. Blanch in boiling water, drain and dry on a clean kitchen towel. Put the almost dry pieces of peel in a small saucepan and cover with honey. Bring to the boil on a low heat and simmer (15 minutes or so) until a drop of the honey dripped into a bowl of cold water sinks to the bottom without losing its shape. Leave the drained pieces of orange peel to dry for a few hours on a wire rack. Store in a glass jar, after sprinkling with ginger. If you can manage, wait a month before tasting!

MARTIN V

ODDONE COLONNA

(1417–1431)

"Papa Martino non vale un lupino . . ."

When in February 1419 this Pope was on his way to Rome to restore, once and for all, the Papal See—which had been forsaken for Avignon in the early fourteenth century—he stopped off in Florence, where the local lads greeted him with the irreverent and loutish rhyme "Pope Martin ain't worth a bean," or, literally, "a lupin seed." Florentines including the Medici family were supporters of antipope John XXIII, and held this low opinion—as low as their opinion of that humblest of Italian foods, the lupin—of Oddone Colonna, who chose the name Martin, in devout deference to the saint celebrated on the day he was called to the Holy Throne, November 11, 1417.

Cultivated, theologically extremely competent and skilled in diplomacy, this Pope went down in history for returning the papacy to Rome, its natural seat, and for bringing an end to the Great Schism, which for more than thirty years had split Europe into opposing camps behind the Roman and Avignon Popes. Martin V was a great Pope and he showed the Florentines (whom he never liked, even when they became his most ardent supporters) and indeed all of Europe his abilities, his unstinting efforts to restore its former glory to the Roman Church. This is why he proclaimed a New

Holy Year, the fifth, bringing it forward to 1423, exactly thirty-three years (the age of Christ!) after the previous one in 1390.

This Jubilee was a great opportunity to exalt the triumph of newly unified Christianity in newly restored Rome, whose churches Gentile da Fabriano and the young Masaccio were preparing to decorate with their masterpieces. With a hammer blow, Pope Martin V declared open the first Holy Door (*Porta Santa*) of which we have certain documentation, as recorded by a chronicler from Viterbo. It was through this door that the supplicant flock of penitents passed all year long. The Holy Year was a huge success, attracting an enormous number of pilgrims to town, with a particularly large influx from northern Europe. Humanist Poggio Bracciolini commented on a "flood of Barbarians who filled the city with filth"!

We know, and indeed everybody knew at the time, that Martin V was worth far more than that lupin seed thrown in his direction by the Florentine louts. What was not common knowledge was that within his retinue, running his kitchens, was a unique character who looked after, fed and served Martin V throughout his pontifical mandate, observing and noting down with incredible accuracy His Holiness' recipes, habits, likes and dislikes—as well as the tastes of the entire pontifical court and the colorful and multifarious collection of human fauna that populated it in those days.

On the death of Pope Martin V, in 1431, this fellow collated his recollections of this extraordinary experience in a sort of gastronomic memoir, his own way of paying homage to his pious lord and master, designed to serve as an aid to anybody who found themselves in this same coveted position or similar circumstances.

In his simple and casual style of late Latin, Giovanni Bockenheym, Pope Martin V's German-born cook, lays out his recipes, no longer on greasy bits of paper, but in a proper book, entitled *Registro di cucina*. Giovanni Bockenheym opens the preface to his recipe book, "*Incipit Registrum coquine quomodo et qualiter debentur preparare cibaria per integrum annum*," autographing his work, "*Jo Bockenheym quondam domini Martini Pape Quinti*."

Leafing through this register (the priceless original is in the Bibliothèque Nationale in Paris, Co 7054) on the hunt for tastes, aromas and forgotten gourmet reminiscences, it immediately becomes apparent that the book contains far more than mere gastronomic curios. Alongside his recipes are frescoes of an age, philosophies of life, histories of the economy and customs, moral and social ideals, all in concise note form, making up a mouthwatering guide handed down to us by this medieval chef in a simple and unaffected style.

The book contains seventy-four recipes, each dedicated to a specific group of people or a social class, providing an entrée to Martin V's pontifical court. Seated at this imaginary dinner table, we can start tasting, in our minds, the specialities of Giovanni Bockenheym's kitchen.

Bobbing in his soup for kings, barons and princes (including princes of the Church)—a chicken soup flavored with prized spices such as cinnamon and saffron—are pheasants and pigeons, swamped in sugar, as rare and precious as gold dust. Gold and silver sparkle on the pork pie, fresh cheese, dates, pine nuts, ginger and saffron, much appreciated by nobles with refined tastebuds. Partridges and game birds, well greased and dressed in spices and ginger, slowly roast on the spits turning in the huge hearth, to satisfy the hearty appetites of mercenary captains such as Fortebraccio da Montone (1368–1424), a condottiere whose ruthless mob made the way safe for the pontiff to return to Rome.

On the other hand, a light soup, such as *stracciatella,* and a Lenten bread and leek soup is fine for the clergy (the lower ranks) in order not to burden the spirit together with the body. Copyists and their wives, however, have to make do with "aromatic" herbs cooked with slices of cheese.

But for Frisians, Angles, Swabians, Saxons, Bohemians, Hungarians and all the rest of His Holiness' high-ranking foreign guests, drawn to Rome by the pious call of the Jubilee, Giovanni Bockenheym sets out suitable, selected foods, prepared and planned with care, skill and respect for their foreign tastes. For example, well-softened stockfish cooked with onions and saffron and spices suits Northerners such as the Swabians, while Saxons and Frisians are best served with pork and egg patties, cooked in chicken broth. Gauls and Angles are perfectly happy with a cheese, egg and bread soup. Great care is taken over everybody who might visit this proto-luxury restaurant, worthy of a Michelin star . . . even people feeling poorly and tired. A light soup of hemp seeds is guaranteed to effect a lightning-fast recovery of energy!

The greatest surprise is that here, among recipes for kings, dignitaries and prelates, there are also dishes for panderers, adulators and harlots . . . As scandalous as this may seem, it should be remembered that this was before the heavy hammer of the Council of Trent had fallen on the Church and the clergy; this was a time when the strictures of the reformed conception of morals in ecclesiastical life was still centuries away. Setting all thoughts of anathema aside, and without batting an eyelid, it is worth venturing in for a taste of the delicacies the papal chef has prepared for these well-defined groups: an omelette of oranges, made without arousing spices, and a sort of almond milk *panna cotta,* very unlikely to inflame the flesh and arouse libido and desire. But who are we to judge?

Sadly, we can taste chef Giovanni's extraordinary dishes only with the tastebuds of the imagination. Nevertheless, they are a wonderful passport into his world, a way in to the domestic economy of his kitchen, so different from our modern-day experience because of the unusual combination of tastes, in which the pyramid of flavors actually reveals the very structure of life and society at the time. Not surprisingly, rare Oriental spices, so expensive and mysterious, are plentiful only in dishes fit for kings, princes and the powerful, as are meats and game, with their symbolic properties of physical strength and prestige, like the gold and silver used as decoration to enhance the opulent appearance of these foods. Wine, ever present on any religious or secular table, flowed like a river into the goblets of guests at the papal court; it was considered almost a form of nourishment, rather than just a drink. All of chef Giovanni's dishes are designed for specific wines from a broad selection. During Martin V's time, the most prestigious wines were from the south, specifically Latin, Greek, Corsican and Calabrian wines.

Naturally, these fine wines that landed at the ports along

the Tiber sparkled in the glasses of kings, princes, dignitaries and high prelates. For the others, lower down the hierarchical scale, a drop of local wine, watered down perhaps, still went down a treat.

✟

Pope Martin V's chef's dishes of the day:

Soup of state for kings

Meat pie for nobles

"Erba buona" (mixed fresh herb) pie for copyists and their wives

Omelette of oranges for panderers and harlots, etc.

House wine: Sorrento Ammazzacane

Vino di tiro

Malvasia

SOUP OF STATE

FOR KINGS

✠

Sic fac suppam honoris: *recipe panem album, cum ovis percussis, cum zucaro et zapharano, et pone panem in pinguedine bene callida. Et recipe amigdalas pistas cum brodio gallinarum, et agresto, et impone pipiones, aut phasanos rostitos, et mitte superius illam temperaturam, et sparge superius canellis cum zucaro sufficienti. Et eris pro regibus.*

(*This is how to make a soup of state:* take white bread, mix with beaten eggs, sugar and saffron and cook in very hot fat. Take almonds, dilute with chicken stock and verjuice, pour this liquid over roast pigeons or pheasants, place on top the bread and sprinkle with cinnamon and sugar to taste. Fit for a king.)

MEAT PIE

FOR NOBLES

✠

Sic fac tortam pro nobilibus: *recipe carnes procinas bene coctas, et pista illa cum amigdalis, datilis, et pineis; et tempera illa cum zincibero, et zapharano, et aliis specibus. Trita illa bene cum manibus; et fiet una pasta dura, et mitte eam in tegale, et subtus pinguedinem, ita quod ardet. Et tunc mitte illam temperaturam in pastam. Et mitte superius amigdalas, et pienas sanas, et quando est cocta mitte superius argentum et aurum, propter bene stare.*

(*This is how to make the pie for nobles:* take some well-cooked pork and chop finely with a knife together with fresh cheese, almonds, dates and pine nuts. Add ginger, saffron and other spices and blend well using your hands. Make a rather thick pastry and line a greased baking pan. Cook this but be careful it doesn't burn. Fill with the mixture and sprinkle with almonds and whole pine nuts. When the pie is done, place silver and gold on top for the desired effect.)

"ERBA BUONA" (MIXED FRESH HERB) PIE

FOR COPYISTS AND THEIR WIVES

✠

Sic fac herbulata pro copistiis et eorum uxoribus: *recipe herbas sanas et odoriferas ad libitum tuum, et pistas illa cum cultello. Post hoc recipe caseum recentem, et tempera illum cum ovis crudis, et zapharano. Et post hoc recipi caseum antiquum et fac pecias rotundas, et mitte illa super herba, et mitte insimul coquere; et tunc mitte superius zucarum. Et erit bonum.*

(*This is how to make the dish of herbs for copyists and their wives:* take aromatic and good herbs of your choice and chop with a knife. Add fresh cheese kneaded together with raw egg and saffron. Then take mature cheese, cut round slices and place on top of the herbs. Cook together and then sprinkle with sugar. It will be good.)

OMELETTE OF ORANGES

FOR PANDERERS AND HARLOTS, ETC.

✝

Sic fac fritatem de pomeranciis: *recipe ova percussa, cum pomeranciis ad libitum tuum, et extrahe inde sucum, et mitte ad illa ova cum zucaro; post hoc recipe oleum olive, vel semigine, et fac califeri in patella, et mitte illa ova intus. Et erit pro ruffianis et leccatricibus . . . et meretricibus.*

(This is how to make the orange omelette: take beaten eggs and as many oranges as you wish, squeeze and mix the juice with eggs and sugar. Then take olive oil and fat, heat in a frying pan, throw in the eggs and cook. A dish for ruffians, panderers, flatterers and harlots.)

✝

We follow Pope Martin V's chef's lead, and end these recipes, as he ended his "Register," with a tip for aiding digestion:

Salvia sal vinum crocus ruta petrocilium
Ex Hiis fit Salsa que tenet precordia sana.

(Sage salt wine saffron rue parsley
Makes a sauce to keep the stomach healthy.)

PIUS II

ENNA SILVIO PICCOLOMINI

(1458–1464)

Bread and cacio *cheese for His Holiness*

The bread in question is Tuscan bread, with its fragrant aroma of fresh-milled wheat, free of salt, which stays good for days and days, the cornerstone of a poor but imaginative cuisine. With vegetables, beans and oil straight from the press, this bread comes back to life in soups, *panzanella,* toast spread with all kinds of good things, and *fettunte,* the epitome of healthy, wholesome and evergreen country-style eating.

The *cacio** cheese (*cacio* and *formaggio* mean slightly different things in Italian) comes straight from the harsh hills around Siena, which turn golden in midsummer sunsets and fourteenth-century landscapes. It has the freshness of *Artemisia absinthium,* the queen of the herbs that grow in these meadows, a plant with hairy silvery leaves and little yellow flowers, blended with ewes' milk to glorious effect. Ranging in color from white to straw-yellow, it has a unique, appetizing and mouthwatering aroma. The Pope associated with these timeless tastes is Pius II of Siena, patron of the arts and a great humanist who, aided by B. Rossellino (1409–1507), chose these uplands, specifically the summit of a

* From the Latin *caseus,* said to derive from *cohaesus* (flow) and therefore curdle.

hill in the Val d'Orcia, to build a city of art that would bear his name for eternity: Pienza, Pope Pius II's Renaissance dream of an architecture symbolizing harmony and perfection.

A lover of all things beautiful, this Pope was also amenable to the pleasures of good living and fine food. The aforementioned ewes' milk *cacio* was one of his favorite things to eat; he had it brought in from the best shepherds in the area, taking pains to stamp the whole cheeses with his noble seal.

Elected rather against expectation on September 3, 1458, Enna Silvio Piccolomini chose the name "Pius," drawing his inspiration, good humanist that he was, from the Virgilian "*Sum pius Aeneas*." His many diplomatic missions beyond Italy made him a globetrotter of his day. In his *Commentarii,* a sort of journal he wrote in the third person, providing a laudatory view of his life and works, he waxes lyrical about the little corner of Siena countryside where he was from, and about how good the milk was from the local pastureland.

He reserves great tenderness for his description of Corsignano, the town where he was born, transformed by a pontifical Bull into Pienza: "*Situm est parvi nominis, verum aere salubri et vino ac rebus omnibus quae ad victum pertinent, optimis*" (Book II, chapter 20)—"It is a little-known spot, but one with healthy air, and the wine and all local provender are excellent." Further on, in Book IX, chapter 3, he sings the praises of milk fresh from the town offered to him by a poor shepherd, who despite the fact that he had not recognized him wished to give him the best he had to offer, albeit in a grimy bowl he used for eating and drinking: "*catinum ex quo bibere et edere consuerat, lacte plenum letabundus obtulit.*" Not only did the Pope slake his thirst on this milk, he passed it around for the cardinals with him to taste.

Enamored of these gentle hills, for which he always retained a great nostalgia, Enea Silvio Piccolomini brought a breath of fresh air into the gloomy, staid world of the cardinals. He was described as a Pope "from the lively lay world" (Gregorovius, *Storie di Roma*), because his background was neither that of a monastery nor of a specific vocation; on the contrary, prior to his appointment, he had led a decidedly secular and reckless life. He was born into a well-established noble family that was somewhat in decline, at a time when tales were still circulating about the Siena "Spendthrift Brigade," a cohort of well-heeled pleasure-seeking young men who in just a few months reveled their way through 200,000 florins (in excess of U.S. $10 million in today's money) in dinners, banquets, debauchery and orgies, prompting an appalled Dante Alighieri to pronounce, "Never was there such a vain people as the people of Siena."

Such was the carefree and hedonist atmosphere in which Enea Silvio Piccolomini, the future Pius II, grew up, that it was quite natural for him to proclaim his early loves in verse,* while rejoicing in the parties and pleasant diversions available to him; at the same time, he set to grooming himself for a brilliant future—though in those days he must have had no plans about sacred vestments, let alone papal tiaras!

Intelligent, smart and, above all, ambitious, he became secretary to a number of cardinals, one of whom, Cardinal Albergati, sent him on an important mission to Scotland to

* He wrote love poetry to a certain Cynthia, a name used to protect the identity of the great love of his early life, Angela.

meet King James I. Handsome, cultivated and moneyed, while he gained an enormous amount of vital diplomatic experience in the northern lands, he was busy breaking hearts too, leaving behind a souvenir of his passage in the form of two children born to different ladies, one Scottish, one Breton. At this time, noble Enna was a strapping young career diplomat, and these affairs were part and parcel of the experience he was sent away to gain.

He wrote poetry and prose with consummate ease, tackling topics that were a little scurrilous for the time, for example his *Historia de duobus amantibus* ("The Tale of Two Lovers"). Briefly, it seemed that he had found his life's calling in letters and the diplomatic service. But his experience as a diplomat in ecclesiastical circles gave him an inkling that here was perhaps a world in which he could excel and fulfil all his ambitions.

He had all the qualities necessary to get to the top in this particular profession: he knew the world, particularly the Curia; he was a good writer; he spoke with wisdom and knew when silence was the best policy; he had a broader view of human relations than others; and he had excellent religious knowledge, combined with an uncommon amount of political and diplomatic experience. Lastly, good Renaissance man that he was, he had a high opinion of himself. After repudiating his risqué writings and worldly interests, he began his fast-track ecclesiastical career.*

* Within a year he became a sub-deacon, deacon, priest, and in October 1447, Bishop of Trieste. In 1450 he was appointed Bishop of Siena, and he was Pope by 1458.

In the words of Gregorovius, Pius II was "the right Pope for a world which had become freer and more human in all respects." For a long time Pius had been dreaming of leading a Crusade to convert the Turks; this cloaked him in an aura of heroic mysticism, which had an enormous impact on his contemporaries, including people outside the clergy.

After ascending to the Holy See, he followed in the footsteps of many other Popes and secured his authority by appointing many of his nephews: he even made two of them cardinals, while more distant relatives and fellow towns-people were appointed to the nerve centers of the Curia in the pontifical state, which was turned almost into a family business.

Quando ero Enea
nessun mi conosceva,
Ora che son Pio,
tutti mi chiamano zio!

(When I was Enna
I was any old fellow,
Now that I'm Pius
everyone calls me uncle!)

This amusing proverb-rhyme, inspired by the great Sienese Pope, is still often uttered in Tuscany to mean that when somebody is successful everybody rallies around to beg for favors. This, of course was a regular practice in the Church in those days, known by scholars as "nepotism," from *nepote,* the Italian for nephew. Tuscan wit immortalized this practice in these effective, if slightly boorish, lines.

So, this bulwark of the faith, riding high on his prestige as Pope-King, and driven by an enthusiastic missionary spirit, tried to persuade Italian and foreign sovereigns and potentates to join him in his plan to harness the power of culture and faith to redeem the mysterious world of Islam. But things had moved on since the days of Goffredo di Buglione (1060–1100), and at the appointed place and time to gather for the Crusade, Ancona on July 12, 1464, only a dozen other ships turned up, sent from Venice: a number of vessels less suited to a Crusade than to an Adriatic cruise!

Disappointment overwhelmed the already ailing Pope. Pius II died just days later in Ancona, his heart rent with bitterness by this shattered dream.

DRIED SAUSAGES

✝

To this day there is still a reminder of Pius II's heroic desire for a Crusade in several Sienese gastronomic traditions. One of these, without wishing to seem irreverent, is the recipe for "dry sausages." Well known since the days of the Crusades, this type of salami looks as if it was packed away with the victuals taken along to feed the brave men sailing toward the Holy Land. Dry, spicy, rather salty, these sausages were said to survive the sea journey very well. They are still, to this day, made to the very same recipe as in Pius II's time.

> Pork meat, very lean, chopped finely, is left for a few days to dry after blending with garlic, cayenne pepper, pepper and salt as required. After making into sausages, leave to dry out near the fire.
>
> —G. Righi Parenti, *Il buon mangiare, ovvero la cucina d'altri tempi*

RICCIARELLI

✞

Another very old recipe, with the flavor and spiced aroma of the Orient, is the typical Siena *Ricciarelli,* made from marzipan and powdered sugar. These delicious little sweets are associated with a legend that goes back to the days of the Crusades. A man from Siena, Ricciardetto della Gherardesca, returned from Jerusalem heaped not just with glory, but with these rather singular cookies, which he remembered having seen "curled" like the Sultan's babouches.

Ingredients

1½ cups almonds
2 or 3 bitter almonds
½ cup candied orange peel
1 cup granulated sugar
1 teaspoon vanilla extract
1 cup powdered sugar
2 egg whites, beaten
communion wafers

Blanch and peel all the almonds, then dry them in the oven. When cool, pound in a mortar or grind in a food processor together with the candied orange peel, adding the granulated sugar little by little. Work until you have obtained a smooth paste. Add to this paste the vanilla, the powdered sugar and the egg whites. The mixture should be smooth but sufficiently doughy to roll out. Roll out the mixture on a marble tabletop sprinkled with powdered sugar until it is roughly half an inch thick, and either use a knife or special lozenge-shaped molds to cut it up. Place each of these lozenges on top of a wafer, on a baking tray. Leave to stand for a full day. Bake for a little less than 15 minutes in a warm oven (325°F). Sprinkle with powdered sugar.

A perfect accompaniment to the classic Vin Santo.

CACIO PECORINO CHEESE

✞

The term *cacio* rather than *formaggio* is used for this typical ewes' milk cheese made throughout Tuscany, from Gargagnana near Lucca to Siena, right through Chianti, the Maremma and the Casentino. Every type of *cacio* has its own secret flavors and subtle tastes, texture and color, which are often the result of ancient local traditions handed down from father to son and jealously guarded like family heirlooms. Some cheesemakers still use vegetable rennet, such as artichoke heart, to clot the 100 percent sheep's milk. To make soft pecorino cheese the curds are broken up into pieces the size of a hazelnut; for hard cheese they are broken up into the size of kernels of corn. The dripping of the whey, after the curds have been set in squat cylindrical molds (weighing 2-6 pounds), is undertaken by hand, or else a special type of fermentation is performed in a controlled environment. The cheeses are left to mature in cool rooms where the rate of humidity is kept high: at least three weeks for soft *cacio* pecorino, but up to four months for hard versions. Then it's time for tasting!

In the old days, in Tuscan hostelries, this type of cheese used to be known as *cacio da vino* (wine cheese), but housewives also bought it for grating over pasta dishes. It is the old-world savor of this "*cacio-formaggio*" (whichever Italian word is used to name it), its whiff of wholesome traditions, conjuring up the memory of green pastures and hilly meadows in flower, that gives it a rightful place among the mouthwatering elite of Italian gastronomical history.

✞

With this great humanist Pope in mind, we recommend sampling quality Sienese pecorino combined with fresh broad beans, salad, walnuts, pears and even with honey . . . and of course a bottle of vintage Chianti.

OLD-STYLE PECORINO AND WALNUT PIE

✠

Before we take our leave, a recipe from times gone by: an intriguing and delicious pie made with Pius II's pecorino and walnuts.

Ingredients

3 eggs
¾ cup sugar
½ cup strawberry honey
8 ounces very fresh Pienza pecorino cheese, sieved
1 cup sheep's-milk ricotta
¾ cup potato flour
2¼ cups all-purpose flour
1½ shelled walnuts, finely chopped, and 12 shelled whole
12 egg whites, whipped stiff
shortcrust pastry for one pie
½ cup powdered sugar

Whisk together the eggs, sugar and honey. Little by little, add the pecorino cheese, ricotta, potato flour, all-purpose flour and chopped walnuts. Blend together and then amalgamate the 12 egg whites, to add volume and density to the mixture. Turn out this dough into a buttered pie dish lined with the shortcrust pastry, even out and bake in a warm oven (325°F) for around 45 minutes. Serve the pie sprinkled with powdered sugar and decorated with whole shelled walnuts.

PAUL II

PIETRO BARBO

(1464–1471)

The Pope with a hunger for melons

It is no exaggeration to say that the balcony at Palazzo Venezia, strictly speaking Palazzo San Marco, has acted as a backdrop to singular events in the remote past as well as in more recent times.

Some sources assert that Pietro Barbo, scion of a noble Venetian family who acceded to the pontifical throne under the name Paul II, and who was a lover of culture and fine cooking, proclaimed from this very balcony the solemn re-establishment of carnival feast days. In 1468, the people were granted full license, though once the party was over they had to purge themselves with particularly strenuous fasting and penitence.

Paul II was a great humanist and connoisseur of art: witness the flourishing of literature under his reign and the construction of Palazzo San Marco as his residence; he also set up a major museum in the Treasury at Castel Sant'Angelo. He ruled the Curia with a firm hand, but was temperate with his subjects, for whom (according to Gregorovius, author of a monumental history of medieval Rome) he not only built grain storehouses and slaughterhouses but also heaped them with bread and entertainments.

And so the people came in droves to listen to the Pope-

King proclaim carnival from his balcony, jostling to try and pick up the coins that the pontiff, a sardonic smile on his lips, threw down on them, causing something of a riot. This was Paul II's way of updating a rite whose fame, many centuries earlier under the rule of Pompey and Domitian, had traveled the world.

This new carnival included major public events: the famous race from Trajan's Arch to the finishing line at the papal loggia, a procession of spectacular allegorical carts portraying myths and pagan divinities, and masks of every type, even for the common people.

The masses gorged themselves on bread and pecorino cheese, washed down with pitchers of fruity and flavorful yellow wine; in the taverns, where steaming plates of tripe and *pagliata* were the specials of the day, there was only room to shelter from the chilly *giannella* breeze for revelers who had a little money in their purse.

Up above, in the great hall, the *minenti* (as Romans referred to important people and the Curia in their local dialect) sat at long tables set lavishly in full Renaissance style. Just as at Italy's most famous courts, spotless white tablecloths and silver and gold ornaments provided the setting for Pantagruelian dishes that gloriously exemplified the fashion for cuisine flavored with cloves and exotic spices and the aroma of the rose water with which the diners frequently rinsed their hands.

The menu, a veritable cornucopia, included lark, duck, roast kid, quail and figpeckers in their feathers; sauces for meats, fish dishes, fruit jellies, *pignoccata* (sweet cake with pine nuts and marzipan); so many courses that the illustrious diners could not even manage half of them. Leftovers were thrown from the famous loggia to the people waiting below, ready to kill to snatch at least a scrap from the Pope's banquet. Being a collector of jewels, the Pope, meanwhile, drank long draughts from his precious gem-encrusted goblets.

Pontifical banquets were a succession of exceedingly rich and elaborate dishes, not just in ingredients but also in colors and flavors. It was during this time, in the many treatises on cooking that appeared in the fifteenth and sixteenth centuries, that the term *flavor* was first defined, broken down into the separate tastes of sharp, sour, sourish, bitter, spicy, etc.

This information and more is contained in a memorable handbook by Bartolomeo Sacchi, also known as Platina (1421–1481), *De honesta voluptate et valetudine* (1474), at the time considered the first true study of diet. Alongside the book's clear invitation to the pleasures of the table, there is also an invitation to retain *honestas,* a framework of moral and aesthetic rules germane to a lord, to a steward, and to a butler, whose job it was to oversee spenders, cupbearers, servants, chefs, etc., and even the cutter of meats.

Platina was also responsible for a habit that became popular at grand banquets of the time: starting a meal with apples and pears, or figs and melons in summertime, to aid digestion.

At carnival time Paul II's Rome was filled with greasy poles on top of which were hung flasks of wine, salted meats, local cheeses and fried desserts, such as *frappe* (fritters) and *bocconotte* (tasty morsels). Starting on Friday, thirteen white bulls garlanded with flowers ran through the city's thirteen districts, while brawny young men chased and baited them in a sort of Renaissance version of the Pamplona running of the bulls. But there were also conspiracies in the air; at least that's what Paul II believed. In 1468 he imprisoned in Castel Sant'Angelo the humanists of the Accademia Romana, founded by Julius Pomponius Laetus, including the famous Bartolomeo Platina, later freed through the intercession of the Gonzagas, in whose service he had been.

Without doubt this Pope, who never tired of reminding the world of the full extent of his powers, made many enemies, but that did not prevent him from doing a great deal for the Church. He set about limiting nepotism, routed the Anguillara family (considered enemies of the papacy), and financed a Crusade led by the Albanian condottiere Skenderbeg, popularly known as Scannabecco, a heroic character extolled in many a Roman tale. His 1470 Bull *Ineffabilis Providentia* established that the Jubilee would fall every twenty-five years.

Paul II came to a bizarre and mysterious end. According to Bartolomeo Platina, by then a bitter enemy, "the night before the Pope quit this life, he ate two good big melons," which were poisoned.

In another legend that circulated among the people, the Pope was reputedly strangled by a spirit trapped in one of his precious rings. However, it seems that in actual fact he died of an apoplectic fit, brought on by indigestion. Such a demise is the mark of a glutton of the first order.

VENETIAN-STYLE RICE SOUP

✢

A tasty and very old dish served in noble Venetian homes, it would seem from the ingredients. We dedicate it to Paul II, who kept up the culinary habits of his hometown during his time in Rome.

Ingredients for 6

5-6 pound capon
4 cups clear stock (veal or chicken)
1 onion
2 cloves
1 pound rice
salt to taste
grated cheese

Put the capon into a large saucepan. Add the stock, a little water, the onion and cloves, cover, and cook on a gentle heat for 1½ hours. When it is cooked, remove the capon from its broth, which should not have reduced too much. Strain it and then cook the rice in this liquid for 20 minutes.

After cooking for a further quarter of an hour, season the soup and serve piping hot with plenty of grated cheese. Our old chef friend suggests, "If the rice is required for an important occasion, in such cases the capon is not served, but for an ordinary family meal, either it is served with the rice, that is, in a separate bowl, or within the broth. Rice with quails, or with any other kind of game or Milanese sausage, is served in the same manner."

BAKED GROUSE OR PHEASANT

✠

A noble dish from the fifteenth-century Curial kitchens.

Ingredients for 6

salt
3 cloves garlic, chopped
6 grouse (or 3 pheasants), well cleaned
12 slices bacon
1 small onion, chopped
1 carrot, chopped
1 stalk celery, chopped
2 tablespoons butter
4 tablespoons oil
pepper
half a glass of good white wine, Frascati for example
1 ladleful stock
bay leaf

Slip a pinch of salt and a little garlic inside each grouse or pheasant, wrap each in 2 slices of bacon and tie with cooking string. In a Dutch oven, cook the vegetables in the oil and butter until they take on a little color. Place the birds on top and brown on all sides. Add salt, pepper, then the white wine. Allow to evaporate.

Add the stock, turn the heat down and simmer for 20 minutes or so.

Remove the string from the birds, pour over the cooking juices and serve hot, garnished with polenta or mashed potato.

TRIPPA ALLA ROMANA

✠

Ingredients for 6
For the tripe
3 pounds tripe of any type
1 onion
2 carrots
2 stalks celery
salt

Wash the tripe well, cut it roughly into large pieces and put in a saucepan filled with cold water along with the vegetables and salt to taste. Cooking time is about 5 hours. When done, cut into very thin strips and place to one side.

For the traditional sauce
1 onion, diced
3 tablespoons olive oil
1 glass of white wine
2 pounds diced fresh or canned tomatoes
1 leaf mint
a pinch of cayenne pepper

Fry the onion in oil in a large pan. Add the cooked pieces of tripe, pour in the white wine, and then add the tomatoes.

Cook for 30 minutes or so, making sure that the sauce does not become too thick. Before serving, add the mint and cayenne pepper.

PAZIENTINI QUARESIMALI

✣

A simple dessert eaten during times of fasting since the fourteenth century.

Ingredients for 6
2½ cups powdered sugar
1½ cup all-purpose flour
1 teaspoon vanilla extract
a few drops of caramelized sugar
6 egg whites

In a mixing bowl blend together the sugar and flour. Add the vanilla and caramelized sugar. Knead together with the egg whites. Leave the dough to rest for an hour, then divide it into little balls the size of cherry tomatoes, and use a finger to squash them down in the middle. *Pazientini* may also be shaped using a variety of molds. Place them on a baking tray greased with butter and leave to rest overnight in a warm place. Bake in a medium oven (375°F) for at least 15 minutes.

BOCCONOTTI

(BITE-SIZE SWEETS)

✝

Rich sweets from days gone by, typical of carnival in Rome.

Ingredients for 6
For the filling
2 cups ricotta
¾ cup powdered sugar
2 or 3 eggs
1 teaspoon cinnamon
2 tablespoons lemon peel
2 tablespoons diced candied orange peel

Blend all the ingredients together well in a mixing bowl.

For the shortcrust pastry
2¾ cups all-purpose flour
¾ cup granulated sugar
4 ounces butter
4 ounces lard
a pinch of cinnamon
3 egg yolks
a little salt
1 tablespoon water

Work the pastry quickly, leave to rest for at least an hour, divide in half, then roll each half out into a thin sheet. Line up little heaps of filling on the pastry, then moisten the spaces in between with a little beaten egg. Cover with another sheet of rolled-out pastry and use a pastry-cutting wheel to make ravioli shapes. Bake in a medium oven (375°F) for 30 minutes or so. Formerly, the first sheet of pastry was cooked, then the filling, and then the top sheet was added and cooked on top. Once it was all done, it was cut into regular shapes with the pastry wheel, hence the name *bocconotti* ("small morsels").

SIXTUS IV

FRANCESCO DELLA ROVERE

(1471–1484)

Herbs sweet and bitter for the Pope

Francesco della Rovere, born in Savona, a student and professor at the prestigious universities of Bologna and Pavia, Cardinal superior of the Franciscans, and ultimately Pope from 1471, is yet another whose life wove its way through politics, luxury, lavishly appointed tables, fasts and feasts.

Preoccupied with intrigue and nepotism, as Pope, Sixtus had the undoubted merit of transforming Rome into a true capital of the Renaissance. He kept up a frenetic pace, perhaps thanks to the dietetic rules outlined by a man called Benedetto Reguardati in his distinguished work *De conservatione sanitatis*, featuring countless dietary guidelines for staying healthy. Above all, he recommended a diet based on bitter and sweet green vegetables such as watercress, depend-ing on individual needs; this advice had many converts among the ordinary people of Rome: since the fifteenth century, watercress sellers have been a common sight in springtime, hawking their produce with the colorful cry, "*Crescioni, crescioni, per chi vvo' ffà la piscia fresca!*" ("Watercress, watercress, if you want fresh piss!")

Despite the luxury of his court, Sixtus IV was not a great eater. On the contrary, he was a confirmed dieter; all the top nutritionists of his day dedicated fascinating studies to him.

For instance, G. B. Fiera, a herbalist doctor from Mantua, wrote *Coena seu de herbarum virtutis* (1498), with a preface by the head of the second Roman Academy, Pomponius Laetus, in which he strongly recommended the use of various herbs at dinner, offering an almost endless list of choices. He advocated similar dishes for Lenten fasts.

Just as interesting is a third work, *Summa lacticinorum*, by a fellow called Pantaleore Cofienza, who restored the good name of cheeses as a substitute for meats, the cause of gout, a disease that afflicted the rich. He particularly counseled eating *marzolino,* a typical Tuscan cheese, made with sheep's and cow's milk harvested in March, as well as *formaggio piacentino,* better known nowadays as Parmesan, of which the Pope was a great connoisseur.

In actual fact Sixtus IV, a patron of the humanists, personally promoted the publication of works like this to set an example of moderation, in a backlash against the kind of books published years earlier by Platina, lauding enormous banquets as a means of bringing rapture and repletion to the spirit.

That said, like any self-respecting prince (such as the Riarios, Sixtus's dreadful nephews who moved into the splendid palazzo at the foot of the Janiculum, today home to the Accademia del Lincei), for official feasts the Pope threw sumptuous banquets where the *pièce de résistance* was almost always a prize game bird, such as figpecker, quail, pheasant or partridge.

At this time Piazza Navona in Rome was known as the *piazza delle erbe* because of its market for natural and wholesome produce such as herbs and legumes. Meanwhile, at a new papal hunting lodge at Magliana, inaugurated in 1480, tables were heaped with aromatic and succulent game for huge open-air feasts, serenaded by the sound of baying hounds.

One such meal, in honour of the Duke of Saxony after a glorious day's hunting, went down in history. The people from town were even invited along, ever hopeful of picking up a leftover morsel. News of this event spread so rapidly that shopkeepers closed up to get a glimpse for themselves. Field kitchens set up on the sloping meadows, in the shadow of cork trees and oaks, churned out an improbable quantity of roe deer, red deer and all manner of other game. Large animals were dismembered, left to marinate in spices and herbs or in apple juice, and then roasted either in pans or on spits. Birds were threaded onto long skewers, alternating with pork fat and sausage. The smell was heavenly, and one can only imagine what went through the minds of the poor, accustomed to making do with potatoes, chickpeas or salt cod.

Another famous banquet, hosted by the Pope's nephew but financed by the Pope, was for Eleanor of Aragon on her way through Rome to marry Ercole d'Este. Nothing was too good for the daughter of friend and ally the King of Naples. The open-air banquet in Piazza Santissimi Apostoli was against a backdrop of *jeux d'eau*, triumphant arches of flowers and myrtle, and fountains gushing fine and noble wines such as Malvasia and Moschatello. Of course, according to consolidated Pantagruelian ritual, an endless number of courses was presented to the dinner guests: roast cockerel, served on its feet in its feathers, spit-roast mutton, chopped into perfect portions, freshwater and sea fish, terrines of multicolored fruit jelly sweetened with honey, centerpieces of fruit and spiced sweets, sauces and coulis, made more digestible and tasty by the excellent wines, angelic music and the perfume of rose water.

A curious little anecdote has been preserved to the present day, nobody quite knows how, which during Sixtus IV's reign did the rounds of all the drawing rooms. The tale concerns an enormous fish head, since ancient Roman times a delicacy reserved for the rich and for gourmands—Luculus, for one.

One fine day the Pope and Cardinal Riario made a gift of a particularly large umbrina fish head to the future Julius II, as a delicacy fit for a cardinal. Judging it to be just too large for his tastes, this cardinal decided to pass it on as a gift to a more important cardinal, Cardinal Sanseverino, who, heavily in debt to the banker Agostino Chigi, thought it a good idea to put it on a gold platter and dispatch it to him. Chigi, known as a bit of a wag, had the fish head garlanded with flowers and, on the very same dish (even though he had plenty of his own), had it delivered to Imperia, a beautiful and very powerful courtesan. Immediately after the gift was delivered to the woman, there was a knock at her door. It was an old man, a glutton and a scrounger called Tamisio, who hoping to get a mouthful had followed that fish head across town, from one house to another. After its long journey, cooked in herbs, the fish head was finally devoured by this most unlikely couple.

The story of Sixtus IV's life is inextricably bound up with that of his nephews. Despite his substantial commitment to defending the Church, Sixtus shamelessly dedicated himself to aggrandizing his own family. Politically, he was known as a martinet, ever ready to plunge into bloody deeds. These include the plot of the Pazzi, in which Giuliano de' Medici, Lorenzo's brother, was assassinated; the overambitious Crusade against the Turks; and his excommunication of former ally Venice, after an unethical switch of allegiance to Naples and Ferrara.

More blood was shed during internecine struggles in Rome between the Orsini family, supported by the Riarios, and the Colonna family. It was because of this climate of violence that Rome sacrificed its splendid medieval arcades, ideal sites for ambushes, to become a true Renaissance city, filled with beautiful monuments like the churches of Santa Maria del Popolo, Santa Maria della Pace, and the Sistine Chapel.

Sixtus IV's patronage and his prodigious spending in bellicose activities left the pontifical state's finances in ruin. Basic commodities such as bread became so expensive that bakers were forced to station a pontifical guard in their shops, armed with a halberd, to put down any riots.*

In order to ingratiate himself with his hungry subjects, the Pope and his terrible nephews reinstated major feasts in Agone and Testaccio during carnival, culminating in events on the Thursday before Lent *(giovedì grasso),* paid for by Jewish universities within the pontifical state, as had

* This led to a saying in Italian, *Appoggiare l'alabarda* (Lay down one's halberd), meaning to set up camp in another's place, or alternatively, to invite yourself to join another's meal.

become common practice a few decades earlier. With great ostentation, once more the carts rolled down from Monte Testaccio, led off by two shiny, washed and brushed—and even perfumed—pigs that the old Corporation of *Giocatori* (Players) had to try and ensnare in a sort of crazy rodeo. Other entertainments for this macabre pagan spectacle were provided by bulls garlanded in flowers, processions of Jews bundled up in brightly colored clothing and generally derided, and masks with all the trimmings, to give the poor people a few days' break from their misery. After carnival came Lenten fasting, interrupted only by a few *frappe* or *bocconotti,* and then the usual evening meal of pasta and chick-peas, stewed sinewy meat and salted cod cooked in every possible way. In the ghetto, the Jews fried their tender spring artichokes and ate *zimmetti,* small unleavened rolls that Christians said were kneaded with the blood of babies.

The dishes eaten by ordinary folk were simple and flavorful. Many of them have left their mark on the modern-day cuisine of the Eternal City.

When he was tired after the Easter feasts and copious consumption of pies, lamb and leavened pizza, the Pope went to meditate at his country home at Torre in Pietra. There he set about digesting his edible excesses by eating a diet of vegetables boiled in oil, and buffalo-milk products.

Thus he returned, reinvigorated, to hatch new plots: he invented the Inquisition (1473), commissioned new architectural works, and found time to celebrate the Madonna in a grand Marian liturgy.

Despite the feasts and splendors of his processions, when they learned of Sixtus IV's death, the people of Rome heaved a sigh of relief, and a cruel lampoon echoed round the city's streets:

Sisto, sei morto alfine: e Roma ecco in letizia
che te regnante fame soffrì, stragi e nequizia.

(Sixtus, you're dead at last. Rome is full of bliss
because of your reign's hunger, disaster and injustice.)

Pollaiolo had created a distinguished tomb for him, "constructed at enormous expense," notes Vasari.

✠

On the Pope's table . . .

SWEET AND SOUR BOAR

✠

Ingredients for 6
3 glasses of white wine
1½ bay leaves
thyme
1 glass of vinegar, plus more for the sauce
a 3-pound chunk of boar meat, or pork tenderloin
oil to taste, or lard
a piece of lean ham or pork rind
salt
pepper
1 onion
1 carrot
2 stalks celery, chopped
a few whole cloves
peppercorns
a few cloves garlic
2–3 tablespoons sugar
a handful of raisins
a handful of softened dried sour cherries

Boil 2 glasses of the wine for a couple of minutes and combine with 1 bay leaf, thyme and the vinegar to make a marinade. Leave to cool and then immerse the piece of meat, making sure it is completely covered by the liquid. Leave to marinate for at least a day in the refrigerator.

Heat the oil or lard in a saucepan; throw in the ham or pork rind and then the meat. Brown well, add the salt, pepper, onion, carrot, celery, cloves, peppercorns and the remaining glass of white wine. Once the wine has evaporated, add enough water to cover the meat, and cook on a low heat, uncovered, for about one and a half hours. When the meat is cooked, remove to a warm platter and slice. Skim the fat off the cooking liquor.

Using a thick-bottomed small saucepan, heat together the garlic, sugar and half bay leaf. Melt the sugar; add an inch or so of vinegar and the cooking liquor from the boar. Add the raisins and sour cherries. Bring to the boil and then pour the sauce over the sliced meat. Serve piping hot.

JEWISH ARTICHOKES

This is a typical Roman Jewish dish, in which the trick is the preparation of the vegetables. Take small young globe artichokes—dark or violet, it doesn't matter—cut to leave a stalk about 1½ inches long and peel away all the outer leaves. Once this is done, use a small, sharp knife to chop across the top of the artichoke head, paring away all but the tenderest leaves at the center. When this process is complete, the artichokes should resemble a flower.

Ingredients for 4

8 fresh globe artichokes
water with the juice of 2 lemons
salt and pepper to taste
sunflower seed oil

Prepare the artichokes as described above and leave immersed for a few minutes in the acidulated water. Remove and dry with a kitchen cloth. Beat them down on a hard surface so that the flowers open up a little, wash them and put some pepper inside. Pour oil into a high-sided heat-proof earthenware dish, and when it begins to bubble throw in the artichokes with the stalks upwards. Once they become golden, turn them carefully so that the stalk is facing downwards. Turn once more, and press the leaves against the bottom of the dish so that the artichokes take on the appearance of a chrysanthemum. Bring a bowlful of water close to the earthenware dish, dip a hand in and then sprinkle a few drops of water into the oil. This is the secret for giving the artichokes that extra final crispness.

MARITOZZI RUSTICI DI QUARESIMA

(HOMEMADE LENTEN CURRANT BUNS)

✝

A dessert for everyone.

Ingredients for 12
1 pound risen white bread dough
4 tablespoons oil
3 tablespoons sugar
a little salt
a little warm water if the dough is too stiff
1 tablespoon soaked, drained and dried raisins
1 tablespoon pine nuts
2 tablespoons diced orange peel

Knead the dough well and add the oil, sugar, salt and, if it is too stiff, the water. When it is nice and elastic and firm, add the raisins, pine nuts and orange peel. Lightly grease a baking tray, and arrange on it a number of small oval buns fashioned out of the dough. Leave to rise for 6 hours in a warm place, covered. Bake in a hot oven (450°F) for 20 minutes or so. If you wish, as soon as they are done, you may brush them with a very thin layer of vanilla syrup.

This very old recipe, typically made at Lent, was, in poorer times, a traditional gift given by a fiancé to his girlfriend, as a symbol of his love and faithfulness. Today, *maritozzi,* stuffed with whipped cream, are on sale in Rome's pastry shops.

ALEXANDER VI

RODRIGO BORGIA

(1492–1503)

A sugar nativity scene for a family Christmas

In the early 1500s the Lion Inn at Tor di Nona, a stone's throw from St. Peter's, was one of Rome's most popular eateries. It was renowned for its excellent cuisine and the finest white wines; its lush pergola of elongated *pizzutello** grapes provided shelter from the dust and baking August sun, adding sparkle and softness to the sea breeze that blows as far inland as Rome.

This inn was run by a certain Madonna Vannozza de Caetanei, a brunette with beautiful dark eyes, a married woman with a regal air who served wholesome traditional Roman fare, washed down with delicious sparkling white wines. The inn attracted important foreign visitors and all the ambassadors to the Vatican; it was a place truly worthy of a Pope.

The learned Cardinal Rodrigo Borgia, nephew of Spanish Pope Callistus III, a favorite of Pius II (who nevertheless was known to tweak his ears for his rakish behavior), would often stop in for a bite beneath Madonna Vannozza's pergola . . . or rather at her house—she bore him four children, and he made her gifts of the inn and a number of houses.

Although all manner of delicacies were set out before him,

* Typical white grape of Rome and Tivoli.

Alexander rarely stayed long. More often than not, he contented himself with a quick snack of bread and cheese, for Pius II had instructed him that heavy and elaborate dishes were not suitable fare for the Vicar of Christ, at least not in public.

On the torrid August afternoon that he was elected pontiff, Alexander VI ate a frugal meal at the Lion before returning to his splendid Palazzo on the bank of the Tiber, directly opposite St. Peter's, built by the most accomplished artists of the time. Alexander had much on his mind: how to get rid of his many enemies; hatch the plots he was working on; and deck out his beautiful children in precious fabrics and jewels—along with his undeniable paternal love, he regarded his offspring very much as a means for conquering the world.

His long-cherished dream of greatness, fueled by an underlying ambition to unify the Italian peninsula, did not prevent Alexander from returning to the Lion Inn and enjoying its hospitality. At a time of poverty and pestilence, Madonna Vannozza was granted a tavern license and waived the usual papal duty, a concession that applied not just to the Tor di Nona tavern but to the other properties that the Pope gave her over the years.

Alexander VI was a lover of pomp and magnificence, who, despite spending much of his time scheming to consolidate his family's power, also managed to conduct his pastoral duties with enthusiasm. He succeeded in strengthening the Church of Rome by refilling its coffers, depleted under the irresponsible reign of the simoniac Innocent VIII (1484–1492), and by eliminating the excessive influence of parasites and courtesans, even though, on the quiet, he did not reserve his full censure for them.

Alexander also built a horrific place of torture, the Torrione Borgia, which was decorated with the sign of the rampant bull, the principal symbol of the House of Borgia. He commissioned Pinturicchio to decorate its rooms. In the meantime, he arranged matrimonial alliances for the four children he had with Madonna Vannozza that were designed to mollify the major powers in Italy and Europe. Yet living at his palace were more of his offspring: a little blonde girl born to Giulia Farnese, who was wheeling and dealing to have her brother raised to the purple, and another young child, whose mother was never officially identified, the fruit, according to gossip, of an incestuous coupling.

The people of Rome had nothing but hatred for this domineering and simoniac Spanish Pope. Little did they care that he had brought renewed pomp to religious ceremonies, and introduced fabulous processions and atmospheric rites. He marked the Holy Year of 1500 by opening the Porta Santa, a symbol of the Church of Rome's ecumenism. The people of Rome looked on him even less kindly after they found out about the cruelty, ruthlessness and torture he inflicted on his enemies in the sinister Torrione, not to mention his poisons (animal and vegetable) and hired assassins.

In Rome and farther afield, people talked of the sacrifice of young Lucrezia, sent off to a loveless marriage; of the family-arranged poisoning of her second beloved husband, a son of the King of Naples; and of the haughtiness of Valentino, appointed cardinal despite his patent lack of merits.

The straw that broke the camel's back was the tragic

incident that led to the death of Juan, Alexander's favorite son and most likely heir. Poor Juan's tragic fate was sealed after a family dinner one summer evening when Vannozza invited children and relatives to her choice vineyard, from where she obtained her excellent wines. It was June 14, 1497, an occasion for celebrating the arrival of summer with a simple meal of early season peaches, bread and pecorino cheese, arugula salad and a hearty family singsong surrounded by delightful gardens, near the Baths of Diocletian. As the party approached the Campo de' Fiori on the way back home, the Duke of Gandía, on horseback, suddenly vanished around a corner. His body was found the next day on the banks of the Tiber. He had been stabbed to death. The rumor was that he had been assassinated by his brother, the deplorable Valentino, jealous of his sibling's triumphs. The Pope shed bitter tears, but not long afterward the swarthy and pockmarked fratricide, who enjoyed publicly displaying his talents in bloody bullfights, was appointed a cardinal.

It was during this time that words began to spout from the marble mouth of a character known as Pasquino.* Hardly a day passed without some provocative and irreverent lampoon insulting this foreign-born simoniac Pope, a supporter of the Holy Roman Empire to boot.

Not that Alexander VI seemed to give a fig; he had a host of loyal troops on call to do his bidding. As King Ferrante of Naples told Ferdinand of Aragon in a letter, "the Pope has

* In the sixteenth century, this torso of a ruined statue, in what is now Piazza di Pasquino, picked up the name of a barber who had his shop nearby, known for the biting epigrams he wrote and secretly attached to the statue's base.

filled the town with more soldiers than priests."

Alexander flaunted his children at public and private functions as if they were jewels. He was intolerant of Spanish protocol, whereby all events had to be an expression of understated elegance. Alexander would have none of that. Official meals with the Borgias were renowned for the elegance of the Flanders linen and the engraved gold and silverware. These occasions were equally famous for the perfection of the highly elaborate dishes, such as capon pie, eel pie, exotic sauces for boiled meats, Malaga wine and desserts.

On the topic of desserts, it is highly likely that the spiced bread known as *panpapato* was imported from Rome to Ferrara by Madonna Lucrezia, who married Alfonso d'Este as her third husband.

The stringent requirements of Lent and feast days, including fasting, had to be strictly observed. Yet between one goblet of poison and another—so useful for getting rid of enemies without leaving messy bloodstains—the Pope had plenty of opportunities to try and ingratiate himself with the humble and powerful alike through the pomp of his ceremonies.

One good thing did come from this otherwise vilified Pope: the Christmas Eve meal. Leading to celebrating the birth of the baby Jesus, the Vicar of Christ was in the habit of uniting all his children around him for a joyful, intimate banquet. Alexander's lover, Giulia Farnese, adorned her glorious golden hair with strange creations, and everybody appeared in their latest multicolored velvet garments, bedecked in the finest jewels. They ate fish and abstained from meat, and enjoyed the many elaborate Christmas-inspired desserts made by the court artist-chefs; little statues sculpted from butter and the *pièce de résistance*, enormous puffed sugar creations following a Christmas theme. After dinner they played games and sang all night long, until it was time for dawn Mass.

Although the Borgia table was renowned for its exquisite delicacies, this is most certainly not the description that comes to mind regarding the dish that Alexander prepared his guests when he wanted to remind them of their human condition: roast pheasant hunted at Magliana, served in human skulls.

When Alexander was dining in public, he did his best to restrain himself; simple salads are more suitable for a Pope than heavy game. In private, though, he gorged himself on desserts.

He was a great lover of parties. There were times when he went wild, such as the occasion when Valentino arranged a carnival party for his father, to which Lucrezia was also invited. The event included a cruel little game in which women of easy virtue were made to race on their knees over a course strewn with chestnuts.

Afterward the Pope repented through the rigors of Lent, eating clear fish soup, pasta with chickpeas and stockfish. At Easter the household ate leavened pizza and made cotton candy for the children.

It is perhaps surprising that this Pope who was so fond of parties was also able to handle himself impeccably in theological discussions and play an important and zealous role in the Holy Year that ushered in the new century. Holy Year celebrations, however, were less successful than hoped; pilgrims stayed away because of a terrible outbreak of the plague and a major flood of the Tiber. Enemies swore these disasters were sent by the devil. Because so much food had to be distributed, revenue was minimal.

Alexander VI, the Pope who embodied the extremes of the sacred and profane, dodged death when a chimney stack collapsed on him during a storm. He rose out of the debris quaking with terror and recited the *mea culpa* in fear of divine punishment. A few years later it finally caught up with him, when the bellicose Caterina Sforza sent him a secret message in a bamboo cane that had been rubbed with the garments of a plague victim. Struck by extremely high fever, as was his son Valentino (in Valentino's case there were rumors of poison, but more likely he was suffering from malaria), Alexander died in extreme pain.

It was 1503. Pasquino commented:

> *Tormenti, insidie, violenze, furore, ira, libidine*
> *siate spugna orrenda di sangue e crudeltà.*
>
> (Torments, perils, violence, fury, rage, lust
> You are a horrendous sponge of blood and cruelty.)

Valentino died soon after his father.

BLACKBERRY SAUCE FOR GAME

✞

This is a tasty and very popular recipe from Borgia Rome.

> *Piglie de li moroni selvatiche che nascono in le fratte, et poche de amandolo ben piste, con pocho di zenzevero. Et queste cose distemperarai con gresto et passarale per la stamegnia.*

Or, in a modern rendition:

Ingredients
1 pound wild blackberries
¾ cup finely chopped almonds
a pinch of ground ginger
2 tablespoons balsamic vinegar

Use a fork to mash up the blackberries in a bowl. Add the almonds and mix together. Blend in the ginger and dilute with the balsamic vinegar. Strain the mixture through a thin piece of muslin.

Serve this sauce warm over roast game.

LENTEN SOUP

✠

Now for the original Lenten dish, a clear soup of ancient origin that used to be eaten in the days leading up to Easter by better-off families as it required eggs, at least one per head, plus fish or meat for the broth. Here is an updated version.

Ingredients for 6

6 fresh eggs

a pinch of salt

a dash of balsamic vinegar

4 cups or so of not too fatty lightly flavored clear fish stock (cod, squid, sea bream) or meat stock

sweet spices (cinnamon,* cloves and others as you wish)

Beat the eggs in a bowl with the salt, balsamic vinegar and a few tablespoons of cold water. In a saucepan heat the stock. When it is about to boil, slowly pour in the beaten egg mixture, stirring all the time. As soon as it has boiled for a few seconds, sprinkle over some spices and serve piping hot.

* Cinnamon was imported to Italy from Sri Lanka in the early sixteenth century, after which it was used widely in first courses, meat dishes and desserts.

EASTER PIZZA

✠

A very old Easter recipe.

Ingredients
1 pound all-purpose flour
1½ tablespoons brewer's yeast
8 ounces butter
¾ cup sugar
pinch of salt
6 eggs
1 cup diced candied peel
lard

On a flat surface work the first six ingredients together until you have an elastic dough. Now add the candied peel. Butter a large baking sheet and fill with the mixture. Leave to rise in a warm place overnight. Next day, bake in a baker's oven for an hour or so. This dish is the forerunner of the modern-day Easter *Colomba*.

To wash all that down, the Borgia's noble wine.

MALAGA WINE

It takes a long time to vinify this wine from the south of Spain, a relative of Jerez, or sherry, in a process that starts at harvest time.

To enhance their sugar content, the bunches of grapes are laid out on mats in the sun and left for twenty-four hours. After pressing and fermentation the wine is divided into three categories, depending on the type of yeast that has formed on the surface: if it is aromatic, it is called *palm;* if it is aromatic and full-bodied it is called *oloroso,* and can be used as a basis for sherry; if it is of inferior quality it is called *raya.* In all cases the fermentation process continues over several years.

This noble wine, made since ancient times, is stored in barrels that are never completely allowed to empty. The result is that the wines of Jerez are made up of different blends. This is a wine with a high alcoholic content, ranging between 16% and 20%. Malaga wine is sweet; it is a dessert wine that can also be enjoyed between meals (Pedro Ximenez).

LEO X

GIOVANNI DE' MEDICI

(1513–1521)

"Palle! Palle!"

"Let's enjoy the papacy, for God has given it to us." So said this pleasure-loving Pope to his brother Giuliano as he climbed the steps to the Vatican.

Leo X was a son of the great Lorenzo the Magnificent and, though from birth destined for a career in the Church, he most certainly imbibed his father's *carpe diem* philosophy ("*chi vuol essere lieto sia*"—"let him who will be happy be happy") with his mother's milk.

At the age of seven he was appointed a protonotary apostolic, by thirteen he was a cardinal, and at the age of thirty-seven, without having ever been a priest or even a bishop, but only a lowly deacon, he was elected Pope. His nomination may not have been a case of simony, but then again it wasn't exactly "divine inspiration" either.

On March 11, 1513, the cardinals gathered after the death of Julius II (Giuliano della Rovere) voted for him partly because they thought his pontificate would not last long. Leo was small and frail, and so racked by aches and pains that he underwent surgery while the conclave was still being held. But his election would satisfy his powerful Florentine family, whose coat of arms with six spheres (perhaps something to do with the "lozenges" they dispensed when it was a family of apothecaries) had not yet known the prestige of the pontificate. *"Palle! Palle!"*—literally, "Balls! Balls!"—went up the cry among the people of Rome when they heard of the Medici cardinal being called to the Holy See. *"Palle! Palle!"* shouted Florentines at the top of their voices in every part of the city, "with great noise and cheer," according to the *Diario* of a man called Luca Landucci (1450–1516).

Rapidly ordained a priest and immediately elevated to bishop, Leo was crowned on March 19 with exceptional pomp, magnificence, solemnity, splendor and jubilation. Never in the history of the Church had there been more grandiose preparations for the enthronement of a Pope. Thousands of artists were summoned to Rome to execute paintings, sculpt statues, build triumphant arches and bedeck the town with hangings of the Medici coat of arms. Nobody had any doubt what kind of papacy the young Florentine would aspire to: he had grown up in a court synonymous with refinement, luxury and good taste, where he had received the best possible education from the most illustrious scholars of the day, including Marsilio Ficino, Poliziano and Bibbiena; the lifestyle to which he was accustomed yielded nothing to any prince in Europe's most established kingdoms.

Leo X was a true prince, a humanist, a lover of art and of the good life, who when he came to the papacy acquitted himself with the style and class peculiar to a personage of his rank. Entertainments, luxuries, hunting parties, plays and banquets were an important part of his life, which was frankly inspired more by secular enjoyment than by the ideals of the apostolate and serving one's neighbor. Not that Leo was ever found wanting in any of his religious obligations: his upbringing and education had prepared him for just this sort of role, and he observed all his religious obligations with scruple and zeal. But it was his passion for culture, for the hunting trips to bag red and roe deer and wild boar at Magliana, and the spectacular feasts he held that left foreign ambassadors and illustrious guests speechless, that revealed his true nature as a lord and Renaissance patron, complete with a court thronged with artists, jesters and whores.

Cautious, extravagant, calculating and dissembling, Leo considered himself a pacifist forced to steer a middle course through the political and religious upheavals of his time. Though he was not known for any particularly heroic feats, he nevertheless left his mark and his taste on his society (this was also the time of Charles V and Martin Luther): Erasmus of Rotterdam, who knew him well, said when he was elected, "The age of iron was suddenly transformed into the age of gold."

Rome certainly experienced a golden age during this Pope's reign. Already a cosmopolitan city, it became the world's stage, where masquerades, miracle plays, services, horse rides, hunts and banquets followed one another in a whirl of daily grandeur.

Of course, as at all courts, the pontifical court used its banquets as an excellent way of exhibiting its power. The degree of spectacle, magnificence, abundance and waste became the hallmark of the giver, and in this game Leo X was never beaten. Chronicles of the time overflow with recollections of these feast-spectacles, eagerly awaited by the common people as something they too could enjoy . . . at least with the leftovers, thrown good-naturedly by the august and satiated guests to crowds of hungry onlookers. One occasion described in the minutest detail, from the menu to the choreography, was the incredibly sumptuous banquet thrown to celebrate the granting of Roman citizenship to Giuliano de' Medici (the Pope's brother), and the accession of the entire family to the Roman patriciate. It was mid-September, when in Rome days are still long and blessed with summer warmth, an ideal moment for such an exceptional event. Piazza del Campidoglio was transformed into a huge wooden theater with seven rows of seating, benches and stalls to accommodate as many as three thousand people.

Luxuriously laid tables were set up, after the altar from which the Pope had celebrated High Mass was removed. Of the six hundred or so guests, only around twenty had the high honor of sitting close to the now extremely noble guests of honor.

Sideboards groaning under the weight of the priceless china assembled for the menu of an amazing twenty-five courses immediately conveyed to Paolo Palliolo Fanese, a chronicler of the time, the full extent of this family's wealth and power, and the luxury and magnificence which marked the celebrations. He begins his account thus: "The sideboard was enormous with twelve tiers one above another, all stacked with gold and silver; a wondrous thing for the great multitude and variety of receptacles of all kinds, for the size of many of these, for the excellent workmanship and no less for its value, for it was estimated in excess of sixteen thousand ducats."

Before going into the details of the mouthwatering descriptions of what the guests ate, it is striking to note how attentive the writer was to the *renso** that was so subtly and ingenuously folded before each guest. When the napkin was opened and shaken out, freed little birds hopped around the table "to the delight of all." It was a real *coup de scène* before the noble repast began, once the illustrious guests "had their hands washed in beautifully perfumed water." To give some idea of what was served and eaten that day, here is a precise account of just one of the courses:

> VIII dishes of cooked peacock, with skin and feathers above the neck.
> XIII dishes of sugared capon, dressed in fine gold.
> VIII vessels with triumphant hoops and gilded balls in the middle, from which rose golden banderoles, enclosing various birds, which, when the balls were opened, did as their feathered brethren had done earlier.
> VIII dishes of mature peacock, cooked, but dressed once more in its skin and feathers, and standing as if they were still alive.

This is just one of the twenty-five courses. It is incredible to think of the appetites, or perhaps unbridled ravenousness is a better description, of which people were capable a few centuries ago.

Our chronicler concludes by reporting that the guests only actually consumed a "thousandth part" of all this food, and

* A very fine linen that takes its name from the city of Reims in France.

in the end, "satiated" and even "discomfited" by the "multitude and variety" of the victuals, they began to fling food through the air and distribute it to those who wanted to eat. As he ran through most of the reserves of the pontifical state in such hedonistic maxi-banquets,* Pope Leo created his very own style of entertaining. Rome's nobles, notables and rich competed to produce new and ever more amazing gastronomical extravaganzas. The Florentine banker Strozzi stunned guests including members of the high clergy, Cardinal Cybo and Cardinal Salviati (one of the Pope's nephews), with a totally black carnival dinner, at which roast pheasant was served in human skulls, sausages emerged from thigh bones, and skeletons with candles set in their vacant eye sockets cast a lugubrious light on the black-clad walls.

Not to be outdone, the banker Agostino Chigi was in the habit of throwing the silver plates used at his banquets into the Tiber (though there were rumors that he posted fishermen downstream to fish them out immediately afterward). Chigi once invited His Holiness to show him the Raphael paintings in the Galatea Room of the Farnesina Palace, his residence at the foot of the Janiculum, on this occasion personally serving him peacock roast according to a recipe he claimed came initially from Nero's personal chef; Chigi himself filled the Pope's glass with the finest wines Tuscany had to offer.

Such was the atmosphere of general gorging and culinary excess during the time of Pope Leo X that even days of fasting

* The king of Portugal sent to this lover of fine foods and stagecraft a Pope and twelve cardinals, life-size, fashioned entirely out of sugar!

and penitence were often hollow gestures. Cardinal Salviati worked out a way of procuring for Lent, for his own personal consumption, pulses and testicles of chicken, lamb, and veal, cooked in butter.

Meanwhile, in the cold and distant town of Wittenberg, a man called Martin Luther, a plump Augustinian friar, was inveighing against the shameful luxury of the pontifical court, and particularly against yet another sale of papal indulgences, a guaranteed fast track to heaven for defunct souls suffering in purgatory, as long as they had a generous living relative ready to pay at least a florin into the Roman treasury. For each deceased in heaven, a florin to build a magnificent new basilica for the Vatican. Leo X failed to take Martin Luther seriously, believing his objections to be no more than the usual ravings of an overexcited monk; he thought that a papal Bull (*Exsurge Domine*), tied in red laces, seals and sealing wax, would do the job.

This proved to be a serious miscalculation. Before a baying crowd in the main square of Wittenberg, Brother Martin started a crackling fire with the Pope's high-flown Bull (the first of quite a few), and not a roast in sight.

According to A. Massorbio, in his book *Storia della chiesa*, the Medici Pope was "a good humanist but poor man of the Church and an even worse politician; he was emphatically not the right man to fight such a fire," which rapidly spread across much of northern Europe.

Leo X died just eight years after coming to the throne. He left behind a poor reputation as a Pope, but an undying memory for the boundless patronage he developed around him, in which banquets played such an important part, providing the conditions for the artists and intellectuals who orbited around his court to create the splendors of sixteenth-century Rome.

O musici con vostre barzellette
piangete, o sonator di violoni,
piangi e piangete, o fiorentin baioni,
battendo piatti, mescole e cassette.
Piangete, buffon magri, anzi civette
piangete, mimi e miseri istrioni
piangete, o frati sprucidi ghittoni
a cui mal la gola 'l gettar dette.

Piangete el signor vostro, o voi tiranni
piangi, Fiorenza, et ogni suo banchiero
con qualche altro offizial minchione.

Piangi, clero di Dio, piangi su Pietro
piangete o sopradetti i vostri mali
poscia ch'è morto el decimo Leone.

—*Pasquino*

(O musicians with your little jokes,
Weep, O violinists, weep,
And weep, Florentines
Beating plates and boxes.
Weep, thin clowns and flirts,
Weep, mimes and hammy actors,
Gluttonous friars,
Cast into debt by your appetites.

Weep for your Lord, tyrants,
Weep, Florence, and all your bankers,
And all other official fools.

Weep, God's clerics, weep for Peter,
Weep, all of you, weep for your sins,
For Leo the Tenth is dead.)

PEACOCK IN ITS FEATHERS

✞

From a period text, here is the incredibly laborious (and most improbable, nowadays) recipe for making the dish as served at the sumptuous Medici banquet. It epitomizes the pomp and gastronomic ideal of the age: the exotic quality of peacock and its much prized meat, combined with the ostentation of gold with its connotations of power, perpetuity and as a portent for future health and prosperity.

> To make peacocks dressed to seem alive: first kill the peacock with a thin dagger pushed in at the top of the head, and then bleed from the throat like a kid.

Following this macabre task, the recipe goes on to explain how to skin the bird, leaving the head and legs attached to the skin.

> Prepare the bird very well for roasting, and fill with good things such as fine spices; take whole cloves and stud the breast with them. Skewer the bird and cook slowly, draping a moist cloth around the neck so that the fire does not dry it too much. When the bird is done, remove and dress in its skin.

Using a special trick, this excellent chef inserts iron rods within the flesh, out of view, which not only allowed the peacock to stand on its own two feet, but even to unfurl its tail. He suggests this finishing touch:

> If you would like it to spit fire from its beak, take a quarter ounce of camphor wrapped in a little cotton wool, and insert into the peacock's beak. Add, God willing, a little brandy or good strong wine.

And simply light before serving. Our chef has an even greater effect up his sleeve, too, for that extra special occasion: before dressing the bird in its skin, wrap in gold leaf. *Buon appetito!*

CHICKEN À LA LEO X

✞

A modern-day French cookbook perpetuates the culinary legacy of this Pope's highly refined palate, with something a little better suited to our tastes and abilities.

Ingredients for 6

For the chicken

1 young chicken weighing ¾ pound
1 truffle, sliced thinly
1 thick slice of ham, cut into thin strips
3 tablespoons butter
1 tablespoon Madeira wine
half a glass of Cognac
3 cups sliced mushrooms
a slice of bread, fried in butter
1 pound small macaroni, cooked in stock
3 tablespoons grated Parmesan cheese
1½ cups white sauce

Pinch and slash the skin over the breast of the chicken. Through these little slits, gently insert the slices of truffle and strips of ham. Pull the skin tight again and press together the open edges. With great care, tie up the chicken with cooking string. Melt the butter in a high-sided pan and when it has started to foam, add the chicken. When the chicken has browned nicely, add the Madeira and Cognac. Once the chicken is cooked, remove from the heat and keep warm. In the meantime, quickly cook the mushrooms in the juices left in the pan. Remove the string from the chicken. Put the slice of fried bread on a warmed platter, place the chicken over the bread, and pour the mushroom sauce onto the chicken. Season. Thicken the small macaroni with plenty of grated Parmesan cheese and white sauce and garnish the chicken.

For the white sauce
2 tablespoons butter
2 tablespoons flour
1½ cups milk
salt and pepper

In a saucepan, melt the butter and stir in the flour. Keep stirring while adding milk. Season to taste.

Even though this recipe hails from France, the perfect wine to go with this gastronomical homage to a Florentine Pope could only be a full-bodied Chianti Classico.

TESTICLES OF VEAL CARDINAL STYLE

✞

Ingredients for 6
6 or 8 veal testicles
1 large glass of Pernod
salt
⅓ cup breadcrumbs
6 ounces butter or olive oil

Blanch the testicles for a few minutes, then make a slit along their entire length and remove the first and second layers of skin. Using a sharp knife, cut the testicles into thin steaks. Immerse in the Pernod and salt, and marinate for half an hour or more. Drain, coat in breadcrumbs and fry in a skillet in foaming butter or very hot oil. Sprinkle with a little more Pernod if the slices of meat become a little dry after frying.

> Serve at table with a fitting degree of seriousness. Your guests will mistake the pieces of meat for normal veal steak, or for kidney. Do not say anything until the after-dinner coffee, then savour the moment of letting your guests know what they have just eaten. Enjoy their reactions. Consider it a psychological test.
>
> —Ugo Tognazzi in *L'Abbuffone*

PAUL III

ALESSANDRO FARNESE

(1534–1549)

The Pope and the sommelier

The Pope in question is Paul III, from the powerful Farnese* family. Mischief-makers of the day claimed that he was appointed cardinal thanks to the machinations of his beautiful and charming sister Giulia, for many years the official lover of Borgia Pope Alexander VI. Paul III was to go down in history as one of the greatest champions of unrestrained nepotism, and he was also known as an incorrigible womanizer. Because of this aspect of his character, he was nicknamed "Cardinal Fregnese o della Gonella"—"Cardinal Fregnese the Skirt-Chaser."

Like his Farnese relations, Paul was an energetic man with a strong physique, an aristocratic bearing and the best education—the ideal requisites for breaking serial hearts. From his clandestine and not so clandestine love affairs he sired many children, only three of whom, Pier Luigi, Paolo and Costanza, he ever actually acknowledged. His lifestyle

* The name Farnese comes from the word *farnia,* Italian for British oak. This tree features on the coat of arms of the town of Farnese, near Viterbo. This area was the location of the Duchy of Castro, where the Farnese had a palazzo and the residence from which they drew their name and emblem, initially represented by a fantastic unicorn, only to be replaced at a later date with Florentine lilies.

mirrored the Renaissance template of many of his predecessors and peers. Though hedonism and worldly pursuits had been a staple of his life before he donned the papal tiara, on the day he was elected, October 12, 1534 (after a conclave lasting just two days), he changed his tune. Not enough, though, to eradicate the kind of life to which the Roman Curia had grown accustomed: under this Pope, masquerades, licentious plays, spectacles, songs, balls, jesters, sundry entertainments and extravagant feasts were safe. All sorts of good things arrived at Pope Farnese's table fresh from his estates: from Castro, deer, wild boar and hare; from the island of Bisentina, pheasants and pigeons; salt-water fish (bass, grey mullet) from Montalto, trout from the River Fiora and eels from Lake Bolsena; onions and vegetables from Gradoli; sweet oranges from Capodimonte, cherries from Pianiano, and oil and honey from Canino.

Pope Farnese was an accomplished connoisseur, not just of fine dining, as demonstrated by the presence in the papal kitchens of the most acclaimed masters of the culinary arts of the time—first Giovanni de Rosselli, and then Bartolomeo Scappi, with their vast wealth of culinary expertise (later collated in books such as *Epulario* and *Opera,* milestones in the history of Italian gastronomy)—but also of fine drinking.

This we know with certainty thanks to the memoirs of the Pope's trusted cellarman *(bottigliere)*: the sommelier mentioned above. Sante Lancerio was his name, and he had the weighty responsibility of supplying wine for His Holiness, home and away. He demonstrated skill and passion in this arduous task, tasting, sipping, observing, making notes, criticizing, advising and, finally, summarizing his vast experience in a letter sent to the Pope's nephew Guido Ascanio Sforza. This document is, to all effects, the true precursor of oenology textbooks, a homage to "the fond memory of His Holiness Paul III, master and benefactor" and great aficionado of fine wines. At the same time, it provides an unusual look at how wine was drunk right across the social spectrum of Rome.

Sante Lancerio's respectful and well-chosen words let us know how many and which particular wines from Italy, France and Spain made regular appearances on the table of the Pope and of Romans in general: Muscatel is for innkeepers, for those who do their drinking by the half-liter, and for drunkards to warm themselves; Greco della Torre, which immediately goes dark, should never be drunk by high prelates but only by servants and furnacemen; red wine from Terracina is fine for notaries and copyists; a true lord would never drink wine from Calabria; and Mangiaguerra wine from Italy is strictly forbidden and dangerous for the clergy because of its qualities in "inciting lust in courtesans!"*

Drop by drop we enter into this bracing world of wine, and into the world of His Holiness Paul III, a man of a refined and expert palate. In these wine-stained memoirs, Lancerio does not neglect a single nuance, presenting an extraordinary portrait of the personal tastes of a man who played a significant part in the history of the Church, and also in the history of drinking culture.

It is almost as if we are by his side, sampling the best that

* *I vini d'Italia giudicati da Papa Paolo III e dal suo bottigliere Sante Lancerio* (1549).

Europe's vineyards purveyed, in a sparkling and costly Venetian glass goblet.

The Holy Father had wines for summer, autumn and winter, and . . . penitential wines for the rigors of Lent, as well as wines to cure minor aches and yet more wines for what could only be described as personal hygiene, for example the much-appreciated Malvasia, with which he gargled, or Greco di Somma, brought in from Naples, and highly esteemed at mealtimes, but which he also used "to rinse his eyes every morning, and also his virile parts"!

Nothing—color, transparency, body, aftertaste and bouquet—escaped the sharp senses of Sante Lancerio, the perfect sommelier who never erred in combining the right wine with the right meal. Paul III could sit back and enjoy sweet Monterosso wine, imported in kegs from Liguria, with a nice plate of sweet ripe figs, or enjoy a bread soup with a glass or two of Malvasia on evenings when the cold winds blew from the north.

But what was Pope Farnese's favorite wine of all? In his heart was the wine of his own land, Caprarola, "because it was from his estate," but his favorite of all was Rosso di Montepulciano, "perfect winter or summer," which "His Holiness drank happily; truly, a wine for a lord." His predilection for this delicious Tuscan wine went against the vogue for French wines, started in Rome by Pope Urban V (1362–1370).

Somehow all these handsome libations did nothing to cloud the Pope's mind, or deflect him from the two main purposes of his life. The first, very honorable, was to attempt to reestablish the union of the Church after the dramatic split begun by Martin Luther: on 13 December 1545, he opened the proceedings of the XIXth Ecumenical Council in Trento (the Council of Trent), to set down once and for all the dogmatic points of Catholic doctrine necessary to root out widespread corruption.

The second goal, less praiseworthy and rather debatable, was, it seems, just as important if not more so to this Pope, "whose love goes out to his own house, devouring his heart," (Pasquino), namely the goal of making the great house of Farnese even more powerful.

He liberally handed out cardinalships, feudal honors and money to all his relatives, nephews and great-nephews. He entrusted Piacenza and Parma to his firstborn and favorite son, Pier Luigi, in the process creating a duchy that was to remain the preserve of the Farnese for the next two centuries. Paul III had a particular soft spot for Parma: in 1519, many years earlier, he had come to this lovely city in the Po Valley as bishop. It was here too, during a solemn Mass on Christmas Day, that he was ordained a priest and first celebrated Holy Mass.

Paul III passed away on November 10, 1549 and was buried in St. Peter's. Pasquino's sly rhymes bid him farewell thus:

In questa tomba giace
un avvoltoio cupido e rapace.
Ei fu Paolo Farnese,
Che mai nulla donò, che tutto prese.
Fate per lui orazione:
poveretto, morì d'indigestione.

(In this tomb there lies
A greedy and rapacious vulture.
That was Paolo Farnese,
Who never gave, but only took.
Pray for him, poor thing:
Died of indigestion.)

TORTELLINI PAUL III

✠

To this day in the Emilia region a recipe has survived for a particular type of tortellini of which Pope Farnese was said to be inordinately fond—the Pope had close associations with this region.

To the refined and worthy memory of a Pope who loved good food.

For the pasta

4 cups all-purpose flour
6 eggs
a pinch of salt

For the filling

⅓ cup chicken livers, well cleaned, cut into pieces and briefly fried in butter

1 cup fresh mushrooms (or the equivalent quantity of dried mushrooms soaked in warm water and cooked in butter)

½ cup chicken, boiled in stock and chopped finely

salt

pepper and a hint of nutmeg

Energetically knead the pasta; best of all is if you can manage without adding any water. The mixture should be very soft and smooth, and the sheet of pasta must be rolled out very thinly, cut into discs 1 inch in diameter, and filled with the stuffing.

Boil the tortellini in good quality stock (10–12 minutes if freshly made, 20 minutes if they are a few days old).

> The stock must be rich yet delicate, for this is the golden rule with tortellini: it must not overwhelm the taste of the filling, or the casing, with a flavor which is overpowering.
>
> —V. Buonassisi

RISOTTO WITH WILD DUCK*

✟

The culinary and historical heritage of the Lombardy region also includes a tasty homage to this humanist and epicurean Pope. In October 1543, sailing up the Po in a Bucentaur, or state barge, with the Duke of Ferrara, Ercole d'Este, Paul III stopped for lunch at Rèvere, as a guest of the Duke of Mantua. For the occasion, local Mantuan cuisine outdid itself with a risotto of wild duck that conquered His Holiness's refined palate and claimed a place among the elite dishes of the region's culinary tradition.

Ingredients for 6

1 onion
2 cloves garlic
½ cup dried mushrooms soaked in warm water
3 tablespoons butter
1 wild duck
1 glass of dry red wine
ground pepper and cloves

* Since ancient times wild duck has found favor not just among gourmets; it has also been esteemed for the therapeutic values attributed to duck blood, considered a formidable antidote to poison (tested by none other than Mithridates), and to the meat (eaten in abundance by Cato to remain vigorous), believed to have strong aphrodisiac powers and the ability to rejuvenate flagging sexual appetites.

3 cups chicken stock
1 pound rice
salt and pepper to taste
grated Parmesan and a medium-sized truffle sliced extremely finely (optional)

In a large deep pan, brown the onion, garlic and mushrooms in butter. Next, brown the duck, and then add the wine, the pepper and cloves. Turn down the heat and, if necessary, add a few ladles of stock to prevent the meat from drying out too much. Cook over low flame for one and a half hours. Remove the duck from the pan when done, detach the breasts and keep warm. Chop the rest of the meat, then return to the cooking juices and make the risotto as follows.

Cook the rice in 4 cups of boiling salted water on a low heat, covered, for 18 minutes or so, until the grains of rice no longer stick together (pilau-rice style). After mixing it with the duck cooking liquid, spoon the risotto out into the serving plates. Sprinkle with grated Parmesan and top (if desired) with the truffle; garnish with the duck breast, cut lengthways so that there is a piece per person.

✝

Now let's hear from sommelier Sante Lancerio as he describes a wine the pontiff was not wild about.

GRECO DELLA TORRE

✟

Comes from an area of the same name, not too far from Naples. This wine is not of the same standard as the wine from Somma. These are wines which vary depending on the year; when not good, it changes color and goes dark; but when it is good it is good, but not sufficiently for a lord, nor for prelates, but for families and furnacemen. His Holiness never wishes to drink such wines.

Pope Paul III's most excellent cellarman also had disparaging words to say about French and Spanish wines.

FRENCH WINE

They come from different places, from Avignon, Provence, Beaune, Languedoc. Only rarely are these wines good, for they are damaged by the sea, they are still murky and they taste of stamped leather, of boots, and of the earth . . . H.H. never touched these wines . . . but they are good for the French to gnaw at their bad temper; in Rome, these are not wines for a lord.

SPANISH WINE

Sometimes they arrive in Rome when a ship from Spain has landed at Civitavecchia, and are then brought by barge up to the Ripa port on the Tiber. This wine is

> smoky and strong, and I believe that many Spaniards who drink water do so to preserve their stomach from this wine. These wines are red and highly colored, and to make them clear they must put in plenty of chalk, and then it becomes very clear and a lovely color, but is most detrimental to the stomach and the body. Whites are rare, and rather minor. Of course these are not wines for a lord, but for families, and they require water in quantities with respect to their greatness. Many Spaniards say they preserve their wines for a hundred years in certain huge earthenware pots buried underground, which is good as these are wines that should be left to them to drink. H.H. never wants to touch a drop of these sorts of wine.

But he loved, enjoyed and appreciated:

VINO NOBILE DI MONTEPULCIANO

It is said that this wine was first produced with loving care in the fifteenth century at the noble house of Montepulciano. This top-quality wine comes from a small area of Tuscan hillsides.

It is made from Sangiovese Grosso grapes, known locally as *pulce in culo,* Canaiolo Nero, Malvasia del Chianti and Trebbiano Toscano. It is a burgundy red of varying intensity, though after aging it tends to take on a reddish brown hue. It has an intense yet delicate aroma, with a hint of violets. Its flavor is dry and resolute, and it has a minimum alcoholic content of 12%. Aged in oak casks, it can be kept for as long as a dozen years, and is excellent with roasts and game.

ST. PIUS V

ANTONIO MICHELE GHISLERI

(1566–1572)

A great chef for the Great Inquisitor

Dominican Antonio Michele Ghisleri, appointed Grand Inquisitor by Paul IV, was a bolt from the blue to the hedonistic and free-living papal Rome of the late 1500s. Strict and intransigent with everyone including himself, dedicated to fasting and penitence, and a scourge of immorality and corruption, Antonio Ghisleri was the son of peasants who lived near Alessandria in northern Italy. He was accustomed to poverty and forbearance, and familiar with the edicts of the Council of Trent (1545–1563), which, having shaken the Church down to its very foundations, urgently needed figures such as himself to win back credibility and trust in the eyes of the Catholic world.

His election, on January 17, 1566, his birthday, sent a tremor through the Curia, which immediately understood what kind of pontificate his would be. Even after his election to Pope, he allowed himself no luxury, and beneath his sumptuous robes he wore a rough Dominican habit. No feasting or lavish banquets were held to celebrate the event; instead, the money that would have been used for such frippery was handed out to the needy of Rome. So, it was *arrivederci* to those sublime pontifical binges, entertaining and scurrilous little spectacles; good-bye to the tempting charms of courtesans, who were immediately transferred to outlying parts of the city, or, in some cases, run right out of town. It was good-bye to cardinalships, honorary posts and noble titles proffered as gifts to nephews or the parvenu of the moment. Pope Ghisleri did not want any nephews around him; on the contrary, he sacked the only relative who had a post as head of the guards for being a braggart!

Not only were the Curia and clergy quickly and strictly made to toe the line, but these new strictures were applied to the citizens of Rome as well. No more joyful carnival binges with *zeppole* pastries and wine from the Castelli, and woe betide anybody who missed Sunday Mass; anybody who dared to betray their consort could expect a public flogging, while doctors were prohibited from treating patients who did not go to confession. (This we learn from a curious document in our possession, an apologia never previously published, which says, "he prohibited doctors from visiting the sick if, for a third time, they had failed to attend confession.")

Far worse was reserved for those who had a whiff of brimstone or heresy about them. Against such malefactors the Pope fired off the poisoned barbs of excommunication—Queen Elizabeth of England was just one of many who fell foul of him—or else he had the fire stoked, kept ready and burning for the stake: the poet Antonio Paleario, suspected of writing salacious rhymes deploring the climate of persecution that lay over the city, was burned alive:

Quasi fosse inverno
brucia Cristiani Pio siccome legna
per avvezzarsi al fuoco dell'inferno.

(Almost as if it was wintertime,
Pius burns Christians like firewood
to inure himself to the fires of hell.)

Initially, at least, Pius V was welcomed by the people of Rome, who were impressed by his ascetic reputation, and by the way he solemnly walked around town barefoot, his bare head and inspired face framed by a white beard, the very picture of a "bold and holy Pope." Little by little, however, this initial welcome turned to dislike and then fear, for his merciless intransigence and the way in which his enforced moralizing turned pleasure-loving Rome into a sort of cloistered convent.

Worse still was that this Pope, who slept very little and ate less, and even then only dined on miserable things, and who had just one sin of gluttony . . . ass's milk (once considered a true panacea for kidney stones, the ailment that was ultimately to kill him), had in his kitchens the greatest chef of the century, one of the most significant chefs in the history of gastronomy. The man in question was called Bartolomeo Scappi, and in the preface to his book *Opera,* published in Venice in 1570, gathering together the *summa* of all his culinary experiences in the service of high prelates, nobles and pontiffs, he heads his credentials as being "Secret Chef to His Holiness Pope Pius V."

Scappi is the only man who has provided us with an accurate description of the complex rituals that characterized the serving of food during the conclave of 1550. *Opera* affords us the intriguing privilege of entering into a closed and secret world to which only the few were allowed access. We learn that the cardinals, shut up in their little rooms lined with purple silk, received food prepared by highly trusted hands in baskets lined with similarly cardinal-colored silk, each one personalized with their own coat of arms, through a special little hatch, and that they were not allowed to receive "closed pies" or "whole chickens." These were always opened and meticulously checked, as were tablecloths and napkins, by a group of strict bishops chosen specially for this function. Even the wine did not escape the eagle eye of these high prelates; the only wines permitted to pass had to bear a name of origin, and then were rigorously decanted and served exclusively in completely see-through glass carafes.

The leftovers from all these many solitary cardinal banquets were much appreciated by the servants to whom they were distributed and who, for once in their lives, had the honor of eating almost like a Pope!

Scappi illustrates the best and most succulent things to cook in order, gastronomically speaking at least, to make the seclusion of the cardinals more bearable. In his own way, his tasty meals contributed to the serene inspiration they sought.

The question naturally arises, what could a chef of such accomplishment, who had shone in the kitchens of gourmet Pope Farnese, who had triumphed in Rome with the luncheon he cooked for Emperor Charles V of Habsburg, delighted Pope Julius II with his favorite *torta bianca,* and fortified the Cardinal of Carpi with his consommé, what could he possibly have made for a stomach that was so lacking in appetite, so unyielding to the devilish temptations of gluttony?

His matchless knowledge of culinary habits across Italy is apparent in his references spanning Tuscan *cacio* cheese, noble and strong Parmesan, *caciocavallo* cheese from Naples, Sardinian pecorino, tripe Bologna style, Lombard soup, Lake Maggiore trout, prawns from Naviglio, and tender chickens and tasty pigeons from the countryside around Rome. He could furnish any kind of menu, not just for VIPs, but if necessary for "the infirm" (to whom he dedicates Book VI of his *Opera*). Leafing through the mouthwatering and timeless pages of his book, it seems that perhaps the only recipe suited to such a singular character as Pope Pius might, just might be a watery soup of parsley and herbs, which has taken its place in history as *brodo apostolorum* because of the way it blends nourishment and sanctity.

Who can say whether this Holy Father had cause to appreciate Scappi in all his greatness, or rather whether he considered him to be the last pagan and hedonist leftover of a dying era? Whatever the answer, Pope Pius V, whose biblical severity was aimed at steadying the rudder of a boat in stormy seas, as the Church was when he arrived at its head, and of contributing to the victorious Battle of Lepanto against the Turks by supporting the Venetians and Spanish (October 7, 1571), "in the end, heaped with merits, was suddenly taken by a crushing pain from his kidney stones, on the first day of May 1572 forced to succumb after six years and three months of a glorious pontificate," as an anonymous chronicler of the time reports.

For Pius V, strictness meant saintliness. In 1712, Clement XI declared him a saint.

Zelante difensor di Santa Fede
Timor non ebbe di nussun periglio;
Fu Cardinal, indi alla Santa Sede
Assurto solo per divin Consiglio.
Dai Principi a baciar lo Santo Piede
Si vide di umiltade un vero figlio,
Ed oggi ascolta chi il suo nome implora
E santo sugli altari ancor l'adora.

(Zealous defender of the Holy Faith,
Of danger had he not the slightest fear.
He was a Cardinal in the Holy See,
Divine counsel his sole guiding star.
The princes there who kissed the Holy Foot
Saw a true son of humility,
And now ye listen who beseech his name
And love him, sainted, upon the holy altars.)

BRODO APOSTOLORUM

✞

In Book II of *Opera* by the great Scappi, much of which is dedicated to making soups from green vegetables, turnips, cabbage, leeks, thistles, artichokes and pumpkins, we came across a soup that, in our opinion, was well suited to this pontiff.

> To make a soup of parsley and other herbs used in the court of Rome.
>
> Take some meat stock, in which you have boiled brain sausages, pigs' throats and spine of mutton, and which is tinged with saffron mixed with pepper and cinnamon—in the summertime, add to this whole gooseberries or verjuice. When this is cooked, take well-scrubbed and washed parsley and other herbs and chop finely to add to this broth; as soon as it returns to the boil, serve immediately with slices of bread in bowls, along with the meat divided up. Note that this soup should not be kept, as the parsley quickly loses its color; note also that this dish is served in summertime in Rome, and is accompanied also by grated cheese and beaten egg.

✞

. . . And the unquestionably Lenten:

NETTLE SOUP

✞

From *Opera*, by Bartolomeo Scappi.

Take young nettles in spring or autumn, for these are better than large ones, and retain the tenderer parts. Wash several times. Boil in water for 15 minutes or so. Drain in a colander, and cool with cold water. Chop and then cook in chicken stock, or in butter or in olive oil or with sweet almonds. Physicians counsel that it is much better if it is immediately washed, chopped very finely with herbs, and cooked in a little stock without being blanched beforehand: the same is said of mallow. This method may also be used with tender leaves from broad beans and peas.

SIXTUS V

FELICE PERETTI

(1585–1590)

Shad for the wizard Pope

An accursed thunderbolt struck Pope Sixtus V's coat of arms placed over the entrance to a shop owned by the Jew Magino, a glassmaker by trade, when, in league with the Pope, he forged new crystal measuring jugs to be issued to taverns, which at the time were particularly used to serving short measures.*

The word went around Rome that Magino was a very close friend of the Pope's because, like him, he was half-wizard. In actual fact, the glassmaker had turned his rare talents to using herbs to make a type of completely transparent glass that would reveal any type of cheating, a practice that had gone on unchecked when measures had been served in earthenware jugs. And so, with the peculiar mixture of hatred and reverence with which they viewed the terrible Sixtus, innkeepers found it much harder to swindle their customers, and the famous *fojetta* measuring system became part of Roman custom, where it has remained ever since.

Felice Peretti came from such humble origins that as a boy he had tended pigs. So energetic, strong-willed, incorruptible

* The measures introduced by Sixtus V are still in use in typical inns in central Rome: *fojetta* (half liter), *chirichetto* (quarter liter), *sospiro* (tenth liter).

and astute was he, that he provided endless, baffling fodder for popular fantasy. For this, he was rewarded with a great store of amusing tales handed down through the centuries.

It was perhaps because of his uncommon talents that the little swineherd, in obedience to his uncle's wishes, became first a Franciscan monk, then vicar, theologian and cardinal. In 1585 he became Pope, "immediately causing more heads to roll under his axe than there were watermelons in the market" (Rendina, *I Papi, storia e segreti*). It was this Pope, so steady in curbing abuses and reforming the moral behavior of the people and the Curia, which in the preceding years had left plenty to desire, who lent renewed vigor to biblical studies. He left his mark on the history of the Church, which he wanted to restore to greatness and majesty.

For these reasons, this rather unconventional Pope continues to live on in popular memory. He seemed to have quicksilver in his veins; in just five years he created five roads, had five fountains erected, and commissioned five steeples and five bridges.

One of the grimmest legends of the day concerns Quattro Capi ("Four Heads") Bridge, not to be confused with the Ponte Sisto (Sixtus Bridge) linking Trastevere and the rest of Rome. It is said that the four heads in question belonged to the architects who had been hired to undertake the project, only to be decapitated for being too lazy to do their job.

Whether or not this is true, despite the strictures of life under Sixtus V, the city began to breathe easy once more after the horrendous experience of the sack of Rome (1527).* The

* The sack of Rome followed a terrible invasion by the soldiers of Charles V, against Pope Clement VII.

city's many taverns filled up as the focus of social life, serving up a light, fruity and slightly sparkling wine that was drunk in great quantities, produced from vines that grew on the ruins of ancient Rome.

An accredited source, *Descriptio Urbis* by D. Gnoli, recounts that as early as 1526 many vineyards were growing within the city walls under the protection of the authorities; the author lists them by district (for example Campo de' Fiori, Dell'Abbondanza, Della Campana, etc.). These vineyards, immortalized in the names of some of the city's streets (Via di Vigna Rigacci, Via di Vigna Stelluti, etc.), bore the name of the families that owned them.

Giovanni Rucellai of Florence, who visited town during the 1450 Jubilee, remarks in his *Zibaldone Quaresimale,* "In Rome during the Jubilee year there are twelve hundred taverns with signs outside. And without signs, an even larger number." Bearing in mind these indications, we may infer how many innkeepers there were who were willing and able to cheat their regulars during Sixtus' reign, and how pressing an issue it was to change the morals of the transaction between innkeepers and drinkers, who drowned their sorrows by glugging down Trebbiano and Moscatello.

Doubtless, innkeepers incurred the Pope's wrath. Despite knowing he was incorruptible, they gambled on the fact that he had a little greed within him and, it seems, they had the temerity to offer a large sum to tempt him to change his mind and quietly forget about these new measures.

Many a legend has sedimented around grains of truth regarding the stormy relations between the innkeepers and the pontiff. All of these tales reveal that the Pope was an intelligent, shrewd and cruel man, who despite his elevated rank had retained the attitudes and tastes of a peasant from the Marches. He always maintained his association with the Franciscan order, and he wore his habit during frequent, almost obsessive unannounced sorties to ensnare offenders. It took very little for a poor wretch to be consigned to the executioner. One day, we are told, Pope Sixtus was walking along Via San Romualdo, today Via Nazionale, disguised as a mendicant monk. He hadn't eaten anything, for in the palace he feared being poisoned by the followers of St. Ignatius Loyola, his bitterest enemies. Suffering pangs of hunger, he walked into the Convento dei Santissimi Apostoli to eat something in blessed peace. In the kitchens there, he came across a young friar busily tucking in to a tasty lard soup. Throwing him a dirty look, and without saying a word, he took the bowl away from him, sat down on a stone step and wolfed it down. Once he had finished, he asked for a second portion. Soon afterward, an old chef walked into the room. Recognizing the Pope instantly, he threw himself at his feet asking for the boon of a fountain for the convent, because his old and tired arms could no longer manage to pull the water up from the well. Sixtus, who was known to smile once in a while, granted his request, and according to one story, "sent his artists to the convent the very next day, and sent so much water that there was no kitchen in any other convent in the world with as much as the Santi Apostoli."

In actual fact, this Pope "who didn't even excuse Christ," and who one day chopped up a weeping wooden image of the Madonna to find the trick behind it (and find it he did!), had fully understood how important water was for the hygiene of a major city, and commissioned drainage of Acqua Felice and a whole system of modern and practical aqueducts.

And yet despite his enormous faith, his farsightedness and sense of justice, this Pope is remembered principally for his cunning. He hoodwinked the Sultan into sending him the Scala Santa at the Lateran Basilica, which has become an object of adoration at every Jubilee, and even managed to trick the conclave that elected him into believing he was an old, lame, catarrh-ridden dodderer more or less at death's door. Immediately after his election he intoned the *Te Deum* with such force that the cardinals staggered back in surprise.

Sixtus V employed a rather unorthodox stratagem to flush out a gang of thieves who had set up their headquarters inside the Coliseum. One night, disguised as usual as a mendicant, he went and asked them for hospitality. He politely offered to help them turn the spit, on which was roasting a tasty young goat giving off an intoxicating smell; in exchange, he offered them a large flagon of wine. As he turned the spit, he muttered to himself in anger, "It won't always be thus, it won't always be thus!" His words later became an old Roman adage: "*Nun anderà sempre cussì, deceva quelo che girava er girarrosto*," which is still heard today in the district of Trastevere, not that anybody thinks of Pope Sixtus. Of course, the very next day, from a window in his dining room looking out over the gallows in St. Peter's Square—every square in Rome had its gallows—the Pope enjoyed the spectacle of the thieves being beheaded, while sipping a glass of Trebbiano wine, recommended by doctor-philosopher Andrea Bacci, along with a grilled shad garnished with field chicory, flavored with a dash of vinegar and fennel.

Pope Sixtus was also very interested in dietetics, a very fashionable discipline in his day. He closely followed the advice of another doctor, Castor Durante da Gualdo, a citizen of Rome who wrote the *Trattato della natura dei cibi e del bere* (1596). Castor suggested regularly eating a nice big plate of fresh cockles, "as their decoction lubricates the body, is pleasing to the tastes, and provokes urination," or a dish of calamari in its ink with vegetables. The Pope's frugal eating habits and dietary rules could not stave off death, which overtook him suddenly one day at the Palazzo di Monte Cavallo, today the Quirinale Palace, brought on, it is said, by a powerful dose of poison. Perhaps it had been slipped to him by relatives of the innkeeper he had had decapitated because, speaking to a mysterious pilgrim, he had dared to curse the wizard Pope and his diabolical glass measuring vessels.

✠

A menu for Sixtus V.

PORK SOUP

✠

Ingredients for 4

1 thick slice of pork fat, cubed
a handful of parsley, finely chopped
1 clove garlic
1 onion, finely chopped
just over 1 liter water
a slice of toast
salt and pepper (or cayenne pepper) to taste

On a wooden board chop together the pork and parsley. Rub the clove of garlic around the inside of an earthenware pot, then discard. Sauté pork cubes until translucent. Add the onion in the parsley, then add the water. Season with salt and add pepper or cayenne pepper, depending on your preference. Simmer uncovered for at least half an hour. Serve piping hot in individual bowls on top of croutons.

SHAD RENAISSANCE STYLE

✝

From a recipe by Castor Durante.

Ingredients for 4
1 shad weighing at least 2 pounds
herbs such as sweet cicely, rosemary and sage
1 glass vinegar
4 tablespoons oil

Poach the shad in salted water for at least 20 minutes. Place on an oval serving dish, after carefully filleting and then reshaping the fillets on the bed of herbs. Sprinkle with vinegar. Wait at least two hours before serving, bathed in oil.

COCKLES FOR SIXTUS V

✞

Ingredients for 4

2 pounds cockles harvested "during a cold snap"
1 onion
olive oil
1 glass of white wine
herbs of your choice
parsley
salt to taste
toast

Flush out the cockles in sea water by overturning the plate they are in and placing it upside down inside a larger vessel. Fry the onion in a little oil in a nonstick pan. When it becomes transparent, throw in the cockles in their shells. Cover for a few minutes. Once the cockles have opened, douse with the wine, sprinkle with herbs and serve hot, accompanied by slices of toast.

CASTOR DURANTE'S CALAMARI

✠

Ingredients for 6

2 pounds medium-sized calamari
equal measures of water and dry white wine (see method)
pepper
salt
squid ink
herbs
extra-virgin olive oil

Prepare the calamari for cooking, making sure you reserve some of their ink sacs. Pour equal measures of water and wine into a saucepan, add salt and pepper and boil the calamari rings for at least 15 minutes. Just before they are done, add the squid ink and herbs of your choice. Serve hot in an earthenware pot, with a little oil poured over.

TREBBIANO WINE FROM LAZIO

✞

This wine was made of ancient vine stock grown inside the Rome city limits. Trebbiano grapes are currently cultivated in the Italian provinces of Piacenza, Brescia, Circeo, Abruzzo, Tuscany and Sicily.

Straw-yellow in color, Trebbiano has a fresh, fruity aroma to go with its dry taste; generally around 11.5% alcohol, it is best drunk a year after production. It goes admirably with aromatic soups, spaghetti with garlic and oil, soused fish and vegetables.

URBAN VIII

MAFFEO BARBERINI

(1623–1644)

Pope Gabella, poet and Florentine
eight Jubilees and a tax on wine . . .

This great patron of the arts was a man whose exalted passion for beauty, assisted by the master artists of the day, particularly his favorite Gian Lorenzo Bernini (1598–1680), transformed the city into the glorious baroque capital the entire world envies. The people of Rome referred to him as Papa Gabella, "Pope Tax." To create this marvel, the Holy Father needed marble, bronze and an enormous amount of money. Funds collected through indulgences and offers during Holy Year 1625 and the other seven "extraordinary" Jubilees, held one after another, were not sufficient, so the Pope began to levy so many taxes on his citizens that he earned this nickname and the following ironic lines from Pasquino, when, to complete the opulent Trevi Fountain, he even imposed a tax on wine!

Poichè Urbano di tassa aggravò il vino
*ricrea con l'acqua il popol di Quirino.**

(As Urban made wine heavy with tax
he recast with water the people of Quirinus.)

* Quirinus: Romulus, the legendary founder of Rome, did not die but went up to heaven with the gods to be venerated as the God Quirinus.

What kind of man was this "Papa Gabella"? He was a Florentine and a poet, a member of an ambitious, rich merchant family from the Tuscan city that, at a certain moment, attempted to add nobility to its rather coarse last name, Tafani ("Horsefly") by changing it into the more distinguished "Barberini." It took the opportunity to update its coat of arms by removing the nasty stinging insects and replacing them with three dignified, mellifluous and diligent bees against a blue background, laid out in an arrangement similar to France's fleur-de-lis. Coincidentally, it was in Paris that Maffeo Tafani—sorry, Barberini—distinguished himself as an apostolic *nuncio,* after which Paul V elevated him to a cardinalship.

Partly because of the malaria that during a seemingly endless conclave was decimating the cardinals* that scorching summer of 1623, there was a rush to elect Cardinal Barberini as Pope, even though he was too feverish to be able to tolerate the weight of the much-coveted symbolic, golden papal tiara. However, as soon as he had recovered sufficiently, Cardinal Maffeo, renamed Urban VIII, proclaimed a series of celebrations to rival the hedonistic extravagance of his illustrious predecessors Leo X and Clement VII.

Rome appeared to be returning to the pleasure-bound days of the Medici, complete with high living, hunting parties, banquets, theatrical spectacles, balls and parties attended not just by high prelates from the Curia, but also by the Pope's favorite artists and poets, keen as he was for some of their

* Doctors' records show that five cardinals and forty conclavists perished in the epidemic.

inspiration to rub off on him. At his summer residence in Castel Gandolfo, remodeled and embellished with a splendid garden, the Pope retired at least twice each year to "purge himself," relax and immortalize in verse the beauty of the place. He enjoyed sharing this poetic repose with his literary friends, along with the more prosaic delights of fine food in the form of edible pastimes of which, to our good fortune, we have mouthwatering evidence.

Thanks to several items of rather curious archive material, such as the daily shopping lists written down as an *aide-memoire* by a loyal steward, unaware that he was leaving something behind for epicurious descendants, we know what Pope Urban VIII consumed during these holidays, feeding his poetic inspiration while fulfilling prodigious appetites and bombproof stomachs.

At lunchtime, on silver dishes graced by the three Barberini bees engraved on the edge, from beautifully clean, perfumed table linen, the feast began with an antipasto of salami, figs, melon, butter and strained ricotta. Next came the healthy habit of a wholesome soup of spelt or rice thickened with eggs, followed by hot pies and stuffed stewed capon necks. This gave way to the boiled meats, for example capon and slices of salami and lettuce leaves, or else breast of veal garnished with flowers.

The boiled meats were followed by the roasts. If it wasn't capon with butter pastry, it would be *mongana* (suckling veal) candied with Seville oranges or small lemons or even syruped pears, or perhaps even both of these dishes, one after the other.

On some occasions, another boiled meat was brought out

after this, and then the *campereccia,* stewed heifer served with artichokes.

At long last the guests could tuck into dessert: *tartaré alla genovese,* a heart-shaped pie filled with fresh buffalo-milk cheese, or a simple *torta bianca.* The meal concluded with "fruits of all types to be found," and, sometimes, with a chunk of cheese.

Dinner was a simpler affair: warm and cold salads, followed by a restrained choice of two meat dishes (veal chops, for one example), followed by a spring chicken or roast pigeon, then by a pudding and fruit. Our diligent steward also wrote down what was on the menu for the fasting days of Friday and Saturday. Meat obviously gave way to fish, first poached, then grilled, and then fried. This was always followed by two egg dishes—generally an omelette and "French-style fried eggs" or *ova sperdute* ("lost" eggs). Served with all these foods was so-called "papal" bread: a soft white bread set aside exclusively for His Holiness and his illustrious guests; others had to make do with "country-style" bread. Leftovers of these lofty meals, swept into baskets and kept under lock and key, were offered to other less important guests at Castel Gandolfo and the staff. No mention is made of wine in these mouthwatering documents, but we must assume that to accompany the fine appetites of the Pope's guests they would have been drinking excellent wine from the Castelli Romani region, already commended by Lancerio.

We have deliberately gone into some detail about the level of everyday gastronomy to give the clearest possible idea of the variety and quantity of food that was served on a routine basis. We can only imagine how exceptional a banquet must have been to celebrate a major occasion at the court of Urban VIII.

Our chronicler also acquaints us with the splendor of two major culinary events during this pontificate. One was a lunch held on October 12, 1625 in Frascati, at Villa Belvedere, given by Donna Olimpia Aldobrandini in honor of His Holiness, which cost the astronomical figure of over 2,000 scudos. Twelve cardinals and massed ranks of noble guests sat around eight tables luxuriously decorated with silverware and crystal, at one sitting dispatching so many delicacies that the food resembled an endless procession. The other occasion was a banquet to celebrate the marriage, announced in all of Europe's courts, between the Pope's nephew, Taddeo Barberini, and Anna Colonna, on October 24, 1627. This nuptial link saw the Pope's ambitious family of Florentine merchants marrying into the oldest progeny of Roman nobility.

The importance of the ceremony celebrated in great pomp at Castel Gandolfo and the splendor and value of the gifts were matched only by the magnificence of the banquet served in the Pope's private apartments, where princes of the finest pedigree, cardinals and their noble kin leisurely enjoyed the finest the pontifical kitchens could produce.

Nobody left the table until very late, entertained not just by the fine food and excellent Castelli wine, but by the concerts and epithalamia read with feeling by the poets who were dearest to the Pope's heart. Finally, the exhausted bride and groom beat their retreat from Castel Gandolfo, while the guests traveled en masse to Marino where, as guests of Filippo Colonna, Grand Constable of the Kingdom of Naples, they continued their celebrations and nuptial revelry for several days more.

Henceforth related to the most illustrious Roman aristocracy, the Barberinis' gilded bees, helped along by the propitiatory "nepotist" breeze fanned by Pope Urban VIII, flew higher and higher, alighting on and leaving their signature on the city's most important monuments (St. Peter's Basilica, Palazzo Barberini, the Church of Santa Bibiana, the Church of Sant'Andrea il Quirinale, the Tritone Fountain, the fountain at Piazza Navona, the Trevi Fountain), testifying to a rapid increase in social and economic power. Cardinalships, honorary posts, noble titles, donations and legacies rained down on Barberini relatives from the papal throne, making this one of the most powerful families in Rome and, indeed, the whole of Italy.

Unbridled nepotism and patronage of the arts were the defining feature of this pontificate. Urban VIII worked ceaselessly on both of these very costly fronts, hence his declaration of eight successive Jubilees to raise the necessary finance. His eagerness belied any trace of religiousness, and elicited Pasquino's typically sardonic comments:

Urbano VIII dalla barba bella
finito il Giubileo, impone la gabella.

(Urban VIII, a man with a great beard,
once the Jubilee's over, imposes a tax.)

The Jubilee of 1625, the most important of his pontificate, attracted large numbers of devoted pilgrims from all over

Europe. It comes as a pleasant surprise to learn that in his Bull *Pontificia Sollecitudo* of 25 January, Urban declared that it would suffice to wish to be part of a Jubilee and disposed toward penitence to gain *perdonanza* (forgiveness). This time, all it took was the coinage of prayer and sacrifice. This meant that the ill, and people in jail or cloistered in convents, could embark on a fruitful spiritual journey of redemption to the very source of Christianity.

So the Council of Trent had achieved a result! But not enough to let us see into the mind of this Pope. While on the one hand Urban, from his Castel Gandolfo retreat, issued a well-intentioned Bull in 1633, calling what appeared to be a crusade to liberate slaves in Africa, soon afterward he upheld the infamous sentence against his fellow countryman Galileo Galilei, who after a trial and a "rigorous examination" (a euphemism for torture) was forced to abjure.

Urban VIII died on July 29, 1644: "The people of Rome, overjoyed, went around town shouting their delight at the end of his blood-sucking nepotism" (C. Rendina, *I Papi, storia e segreti*).

WHEAT SOUP

✝

From the Castel Gandolfo holiday menu we have selected a tasty wheat soup that, good Tuscan that he was, His Holiness would almost certainly have enjoyed. We offer two versions of this soup. The first is taken from *Panunto Toscano* (1705), by the Florentine Jesuit Francesco Gaudenzio, a renowned food lover and painstaking observer of traditional and inexpensive cuisine.

> To make wheat soup:
>
> Check through the wheat and wash in warm water: for ten persons, one and a half bowlfuls will suffice. Cook in ordinary hot and fatty stock; you will be adding more stock little by little, stirring occasionally with a wooden spoon, simmering on a low heat—the longer it cooks, the better it gets. Note that it needs to simmer for at least three and a half hours. When you think it is ready, finely chop a little pork fat—make sure it is not rancid—and delicately melt in a frying pan. Pour over the wheat and, to finish, add eggs and mild cheese. If desired, a drop of vinegar adds a splash of color.
>
> —F. Gaudenzio, *Panunto*

The second is an up-to-date descendant of the first recipe, the pride of cooking in and around the Tuscan city of Lucca.

Ingredients for 6

16 ounces borlotti beans, soaked in water, covered, and left overnight
a sprig of rosemary
a pinch of salt
a few cloves of garlic
1 pig's knuckle, washed well, scraped and cut lengthways in two
1 stalk celery
1 carrot
1 onion
1 small slice pork fat, chopped
½ cup whole wheat grain
1 cup stock
half a glass of olive oil
pepper to taste

Drain the beans and cook them in fresh water in a pot, preferably earthenware, with the rosemary, salt and garlic. Add the pig's knuckle and simmer for over an hour. Meanwhile sauté the celery, carrot and onion in the pork fat. When the knuckle is cooked, remove it, put the beans through a masher and return to the stock. Add the vegetable mixture and the spelt, incorporate the stock and salt and cook for at least another hour. If the soup is too thick, you can add a ladle or two of water.

Serve with a drizzle of top-quality olive oil and a pinch of freshly ground black pepper.

OVA SPERDUTE

(LOST EGGS)

✝

Now, from the papal menu, "lost eggs" for Fridays, forerunner of modern-day poached eggs. This is how an olden-day cookbook suggests we proceed.

> Bring the water to the boil and break very fresh eggs into it. As soon as they are set, remove from the water while still tender, and sprinkle over sugar, rose water, sweet spices, and a little juice from an orange or unripe fruit. If you like, instead of the above ingredients sprinkle with good grated cheese and sweet spices.

TORTA BIANCA

✟

To conclude, a slice of *torta bianca* and a nice glass of wine made from Castel Gandolfo's very own vines. This is an updated version of a very old recipe by Messimburgo, the great chef of the Este court in the sixteenth century.

For the flaky pastry
1½ cups all-purpose flour
6 tablespoons butter or margarine
⅓ cup granulated sugar
a pinch of salt
1 egg yolk
2–3 tablespoons rose water

For the filling
4 egg whites
⅓ cup and 1 tablespoon granulated sugar
4–5 tablespoons rose water
1 cup heavy cream
powdered sugar

Use the pastry to line a high-sided buttered cake pan.

Preheat the oven to 425°F and begin to make the filling. Whip the egg whites until they are very stiff, adding the granulated sugar little by little carefully so that they retain their stiffness; lastly, incorporate the rose water. Very slowly amalgamate the cream, making sure that the egg whites do not start to go runny.

Carefully fill the pastry mold and then bake for 40 minutes or so.

This *torta* rises and goes a lovely golden brown color. When it has cooled and settled, sprinkle with plenty of powdered sugar.

CASTEL GANDOLFO WINE

✠

"There is not much of it and it is of exclusive output, but it is exceedingly perfect, especially for the summer. But it must not be moved from where it is made, for when it is down in the plain, where the breeze does not pass, it changes and alters. His Holiness sometimes drank these wines when he was at Castel Gandolfo."

—Sante Lancerio, cellarman to Paul III

PIUS VI

GIOVANNI ANGELO BRASCHI

(1775–1799)

The Pope with the flowing locks and dainty feet

On his travels through Italy in 1786, Goethe found time between a nice glass of white wine in the Castelli Romani and a love affair to describe the Pope in particular detail, as "the most handsome and worthy figure of a man of the age."

Pius VI, scion of the noble Braschi family of Romagna, elected Pope after a long and stormy conclave (February 15, 1775), and the butt of many pasquinades—as Pasquino's lampoons were called—was tall and handsome and wore his hair long, in the fashion of the day. Brought up as any young lord was, he suffered the telling weakness of fussily showing off his very dainty and very small feet as he was driven through the streets of Rome in his carriage, to the great mirth of the common people.

His papal tables, decked out in typical eighteenth-century luxury and refinement, featured obscure and intriguing dishes: chocolate delicacies, poultry steeped in herbs and then roasted, and then a drop of coffee as a digestive, taken daily in Rome's first café, commissioned and built in the Vatican Gardens by Benedict XIV, one of Pius VI's predecessors.

Pope Braschi believed that a real Pope should act like a king. But times were changing, and just around the corner lay tragic events that would usher in a new European order and dash his dreams.

Such was the revolutionary momentum sweeping the Continent that even the most conservative emperors took anticlerical measures. An example was Joseph II, the Holy Roman Emperor, who suppressed the Society of Jesus and the contemplative orders, and proclaimed his Edict of Toleration for religious minorities.

This poor Pope, who wanted to distinguish Rome as Europe's most high-spirited principality, used luxury as a showy diversion to maintain good relations with those sovereigns who strove to seem as though they were keeping up with the times, whatever the cost. All his efforts were in vain. His biggest blow was promulgation of the Civil Constitution of the Clergy (1790), which reformed the Church in France and marked the beginning of his tragic decline.

He most certainly had no inkling of the tragic fate that awaited him when, in 1773 as newly elected Pope, richly dressed in fine vestments, he launched Holy Year celebrations by opening the *Porta Santa*. His long life's journey took him from Siena—where in his irreverent memory there is a tavern called La Pisciata del Papa ("The Pope's Piss")—to Florence, Turin and ultimately to Valence.

In the succeeding months, although the Pope did officiate at spectacular and solemn Masses, he indulged in worldly events of uncommon magnificence—balls, processions and banquets—in a questionable mixture of sacred and profane.

* At this locale a plaque notes: "Obeying the call of nature, the Pope stopped here."

Detractors claimed that this was the Pope's way of trying to avert the fast-approaching specter of revolution.

After prayer, the Pope and his court often entertained illustrious foreign guests, such as Archduke Maximilian of Austria, brother of the terrible Joseph, with feasts that lasted all night long. On tables decked out with the utmost finery, set out on vast quantities of French lace, the high points of these banquets were of course the meat dishes, served with the latest French-style sauces, as well as meat pies and stews, and tasty chocolate and coffee delights, presented in elegant Sèvres cups, wonders of an epoch so rich in political, cultural and gastronomic ferment.

One papal subject, a certain Antonio Nebbia of Macerata, published a much-vaunted guide to upper-class cooking, *Cucina teorico pratica,* in which, for the first time in Italy, mention was made of sauces invented by the famous La Varenne. The book also included a recipe for *princisgras* (later standardized as *vincisgrassi*), a sort of pie with a meat sauce incorporating chicken giblets, also known today as Marches-style lasagne.

Rome's fashionable celebrations for the Jubilee featured illuminations, pyrotechnics, old-fashioned Barbary horse races, and gurgling fountains with gargoyle spouts issuing fine Castelli wine, all to the sound of harpsichords and spinets playing minuets.

When the Jubilee celebrations were over, the Pope put the finishing touches to several ambitious projects he hoped would allow him to keep abreast of the changing times, but which almost bankrupted the already financially imperiled state. However, all the while, on the sly he was enriching the nephews with whom he went hunting for pheasants and grouse at the Magliana estate—birds that were later stewed by his masterly chefs, using the old recipe from the *Panunto.*

Pius VI began implementing his grandiose plan to drain the Pontine marshes as a way of providing good new land for farmers and wiping out malaria; he raised obelisks, founded the splendid Pius–Clementine Museum, and surrounded himself with the crème de la crème of intellectual society, including Goethe. In preference to the magnificent residence at Castel Gandolfo, this Pope holidayed at the castle in Terracina, from where he could keep a firsthand watch on the progress of the marsh-draining project.

At this time, the Castelli Romani just south of Rome had become a favored haunt for bandits, but this did nothing to dissuade intellectuals on the Grand Tour from visiting the area. They came to dabble in poetry and music, and went mushroom hunting in the virgin woods, bountifully stocked with ovoli and porcini mushrooms. Their woodland trophies were then served up in the local taverns as salads or on fresh egg fettuccine, alongside ricotta cheese and pecorino, matured in the local tufa cellars. We have Goethe's word that, for many, a pastoral love affair was part of the experience!

Alas, the poor Pope had to forgo all this luxury. Whether he was at the castle at Terracina or resident at the Roman See, he was threatened not only by popular uprisings, but by French invaders. Worse, he had been picked out as an object of ridicule by all and sundry, even by de Sade, who in his *Histoire de Juliette* accused him of making devilish use of black masses. The simple truth is that Pope Pius VI was a very ambitious man, whose penchant for frivolities and earthly pleasures—the result of his family upbringing—rankled with the changing times.

As soon as the lights were dimmed on the 1793 festivities, the people followed the example of their French counterparts and rose up in a bloody revolution. The Pope's carriage was stoned, and he was stabbed—but not fatally.

More tortuous and tragic events ensued to bring Pope Braschi's tumultuous pontificate to an end. What awaited him was a long journey, during which imprisonment, beatings and hardships took their toll. By the time he arrived in Valence, in France, he was so weak that he passed away as he was being taken down from the sedan chair.

Pasquino, as ever, was ready with an epitaph:

Un Pio perde la fede
per conservar la sede.

(A Pius loses his faith
to hang on to his throne.)

VINCISGRASSI

(PASTA)

✠

An historical dish recorded in recipe form during Pius VI's time. Here is a modernized version.

Ingredients for 6–8

3⅓ cups all-purpose flour
2 eggs and 1 egg yolk
1 tablespoon olive oil
salt to taste
1 spring onion
1 carrot
1 stalk celery
1 tablespoon butter
6 ounces minced beef
salt and pepper
stock
4 ounces chicken giblets
a few bay leaves
1 clove
1 tablespoon flour
1 small black truffle, very finely sliced
1 cup grated Parmesan cheese
4 tablespoons butter

Heap up the flour on a board, make a well and pour into this the eggs and the extra egg yolk, oil, salt, and a few tablespoons of water. Work the pasta vigorously and then leave to rest for a few minutes before rolling it out into a flat sheet. Meanwhile, prepare the sauce: chop up the spring onion, carrot and celery and brown in the butter. Add the meat, season with salt and pepper and pour in a little stock.

Cover and cook on a low heat for an hour or so. Ten minutes before it is ready, add the chicken giblets, bay leaves, clove and flour, stirring frequently from this point onward. Cut the pasta into squares. Boil. Cook 8-10 minutes. Drain while still *al dente,* and then make layers in an oven-proof dish, alternating with meat sauce; sprinkle each layer with truffle and Parmesan. Finish with a layer of pasta, drench in melted butter and sprinkle with Parmesan cheese. Bake in a hot oven at 450°F for 20 minutes.

STEWED GROUSE OR PHEASANT

✠

The Papal Curia perpetuated many traditional recipes, particularly those for game. Here is a very old recipe, as described in the *Panunto*.

Ingredients for 4

4 cleaned, plucked and gutted grouse or pheasants
1 beef marrowbone
1 cinnamon stick
1 tablespoon vinegar
a pinch of sugar
salt to taste
2 quinces, sliced
4 plums
a handful of dried sour cherries
half a glass of dry Castelli white wine
grilled polenta

Place the birds in a Dutch oven. Add the beef marrow, cinnamon, vinegar, sugar and salt and cover in cold water. Bring to the boil and then simmer on a low heat. Skim the surface. When no more scum rises to the surface, add the fruit and wine. Simmer for about an hour, covered, and serve piping hot with slices of grilled polenta.

SALAD OF CASTELLI OVOLI MUSHROOMS AND PECORINO ROMANO CHEESE

✝

The forest around the Castelli Romani, like the woods at Oriolo and Manziana, is prime ovoli and porcini mushroom territory. Intellectuals on the Grand Tour did more than just look at ruins when they passed through this area. Here is a very tasty, refined and luxurious dish, already a delicacy in the olden days, which modern chefs prepare as follows.

Ingredients for 6

6 nice fresh ovoli mushrooms (it is very important that they are extremely fresh)
extra-virgin olive oil
juice of 1 lemon
salt
pepper to taste
roughly 6 ounces medium-strength pecorino Romano cheese, in flakes

Carefully clean the ovoli mushrooms with a damp cloth. Slice thinly, if possible vertically, so that the slices retain their mushroom shape. Arrange the slices on an oval serving dish without overlapping. Pour over a vinaigrette made with a little extra-virgin olive oil beaten together with lemon juice, salt, and pepper. Place slivers of pecorino cheese on top of the mushrooms and serve. Makes a delicious antipasto or a dish to be eaten between courses.

GREGORY XVI

BARTOLOMEO ALBERTO CAPPELLARI

(1831–1846)

Gone fishing . . .

Every year, Pope Gregory XVI was taken in the same carriage to his holiday residence at Castel Gandolfo, on the way passing decorations and triumphant arches ornamented not just with greenery but with neoclassical monumental columns, statues and honorific epigraphs. He claimed that he was too old for the train, and consequently decided to leave it to his successor to inaugurate this new form of locomotion. This upset many self-proclaimed modern men, including the poet Carducci, who regarded this Pope as a reactionary and enemy of progress.

At this pleasant retreat, far from the bustle of the capital city and the explosions set by revolutionaries in Romagna and elsewhere, the Pope could pray, rest and fish to his heart's desire; his catch of freshwater fish, often the most humble of species, could almost suffice to feed much of the Curia.

A Camaldolese* monk in his younger days, though cheerful by nature and a man who liked a good joke, Pope Gregory XVI was always a little shy and reserved. It was thus no surprise that he enjoyed shutting himself away in the

* An order of monks formed at Camaldoli (Arezzo, Italy) in the eleventh century.

Castel Gandolfo villa overlooking the lake, splendid and welcoming once more after centuries of neglect. To ensure the greatest possible privacy, he dodged any bores lying in wait by using the tradesmen's entrance.

He did his best to elude the sumptuous receptions thrown in his honor by local notables. He far preferred going on pastoral visits to the nearby towns of Velletri, Grottaferrata and Frascati. On these trips he sat down to eat with parish priests and monks, and was perfectly happy with cheese and refried chicory, a legacy of his loyalty to the Camaldolese rule.

He always left on foot, grumbling at the chief groom who was huffing and puffing to keep up with the Pope's fast pace while considerately attempting to keep the sun off his head with a parasol.

When he managed to free himself from pastoral commitments, ceremonies, prayers, meetings with ambassadors and all the rest, there was nothing he liked better than to take a boat out into the middle of the lake. Fishing was his passion—as if he was St. Peter brought back to life—and he was such a skillful angler that he never came back empty-handed. Perhaps this was why, at a time of poverty such as the mid-nineteenth century, Gregory naively wanted to feed the Curia with his own haul.

Belli paints a fairly true-to-life portrait, describing him as the Pope "who fished tench for fasting" and was happy on holiday when, at home, "there wasn't so much as a penny to be found."

Perhaps the Pope used his time on the lake as a way of dreaming up some kind of solution to the enormous financial and political problems that beset his state: how to roll back the revolution in Romagna, how to turn the finances round, and how to ward off the specter of cholera, which was claiming so many lives.

He increased the tax on wine (1846) and heightened fiscal pressure, both highly unpopular measures that triggered off popular anger, particularly among the poor. People began to speak ill of him. And yet the Pope did not seem to take this too personally. On the contrary, he continued to play memorable practical jokes on his friends, as when he was out walking with cardinals in the Vatican Gardens, and, chatting away, led them beneath the jets of a fountain; or when he slipped roast chickens, done to a turn, into the cardinals' capacious pockets.

In his own way, Pope Gregory XVI was a generous man. It is recorded that in July 1845 he sent an enormous carp that he had personally fished from one of the big tanks in his gardens, packed in flowers and lemons, to newly appointed Cardinal Caraffa di Traetto. He also donated fruit left over from his meals to an old Camaldolese friar called Fortunato, whom he came across one day quite by chance at the Frascati hermitage; a boatman in Venice by trade, when the Pope had been a young man, the friar had rescued him from certain death one day as he got into difficulties swimming in the Venice lagoon.

Pope Cappellari very much enjoyed living outside Rome; when he was in town, he sought consolation by going on such long walks that he tired out the fittest of his dignitaries. He required very little persuasion to embark on any possible journey, especially if the destination was graced with a body of water nearby.

One day he went on a visit to San Felice Circeo and Terracina. As well as the religious chants, pious Masses and grandiose illuminations simulating waterborne fires, he was attended by a barge rigged out with flowers and white fabric, which took him and his cardinal brother out onto Lake Paola. To the sweet strains of accompanying instrumental music, he enjoyed a glorious day's fishing. This was in 1839, a year when the Pope only just escaped a fiery cannonball that—nobody ever satisfactorily explained how—had erroneously been fired in his direction from the town fortress. In the meantime, the people's mutterings grew more vociferous, even though he had shrewdly abolished publication of the names of people who had not observed Easter. This measure helped to reestablish some degree of religious fervor. More people began to observe Easter and Friday fasting, occasions that nonetheless were quickly forgotten when the capital dedicated itself to extravagant Saturday night feasts, known as *Sabbatine*.

The situation continued to deteriorate for the public purse, and the people began openly to voice their discontent with the Pope. They smirked wickedly at the thought of this jovial and chubby man enjoying long naps with the wife of his faithful servant Gaetaninon—the lovely Clementina, like her husband, died exceedingly rich, according to Belli in his irreverent sonnet "Er Papa omo," a view also expounded by Stendhal in a memorable letter.

The Pope was criticized from all sides: for being a spendthrift, for helping relatives, for failing to respect etiquette when he halted processions in order to exchange a kindly word with the little girls who scattered flower petals; he was even condemned one day in Tivoli for being charitable and donating to the poor a triumphal arch made out of splendid bunches of *pizzutella* grapes that the citizens had erected for him.

The talk turned more and more unpleasant, despite the fact that during his pontificate Gregory zealously protected the faith from the onslaught of materialist positivism (his 1832 encyclical *Mirari vos*), and extended ecumenism through a concerted strategy of missions. As the deficit piled up, partly because of the costs of paying for French and Austrian garrisons to protect the people of Romagna from the rebellious patriots, the backbiting degenerated into uprisings.

All the Pope could do to console himself was go fishing.

He spent his last day as a free man, a windy day blowing no one any good, at Baron Grazioli's estate at Castel Porziano. For this splendid feast his host had enclosed a stretch of sea containing all sorts of fish, so that the Holy Father could enjoy himself as much as possible. The Pope was transported to the spot in a flotilla of boats; despite the strong winds, he had a very successful fishing expedition. Afterward, he sat down to a lavish banquet of fresh fish, and overturned etiquette by asking for the old Baroness to sit next to him—no women were actually allowed at the table. Back in Rome, gossiping tongues commented that the two bakers had got on like a house on fire, a reference to their humble origins as bakers' sons.

Gregory returned to Rome to his offices, humble habits and frugal meals. Although he was visibly wasting away, he refused to consult his chief physician because he did not want to burden the state treasury; he didn't summon a doctor of any kind, and his strong constitution was overwhelmed in just a few days, probably by cancer.

✝

Here are some tasty ways to cook the humble fish to which Gregor XVI was so partial.

STEWED TENCH WITH PEAS (FRESHWATER FISH SUCH AS CARP OR TROUT)

✠

Ingredients for 4

1 shallot
olive oil as required
4 fresh tomatoes, diced
4 medium-sized tench (around ½ pound each), cleaned and dried
1 glass of dry white wine
1 pound fresh shelled peas
salt and pepper
toast

Slice the shallot and fry in oil in a nonstick pan with fairly high sides. Add the tomatoes and whole fish, side by side. After 20 minutes or so on a low heat, cover and bathe with the white wine. Throw in the peas. Season with salt and pepper and cook for 15 minutes more, checking to make sure that the fish does not stick to the pan. If the sauce becomes too thick, add a little water. Serve hot with toast.

SOUSED CARP

This very old recipe, used especially with large and bony freshwater fish, is a good way of preserving them for a few days. It can also be used with fish typically found in the Tiber, such as roach or barbel.

Ingredients for 6
1 carp (at least 3 pounds)
½ cup flour
vegetable oil
salt
glass of warm red vinegar
1 clove of garlic
pepper
a few mint leaves
a handful of chopped parsley
olive oil

Clean the carp, scale, rinse and cut into square pieces. Pat dry, dip in flour and fry in oil in a nonstick pan. When all the pieces are nicely browned, arrange them on an oval serving dish. Season with salt, garlic, pepper and mint.

Leave to macerate for at least 24 hours. Before serving, sprinkle over the parsley and bathe with a few tablespoons of olive oil.

RAW FIELD CHICORY

✠

Chicory concluded evenings of penitence and fasting. This is a very old Roman dish, typically eaten during Easter fasting.

Ingredients for 4

2 pounds tender fresh spring field chicory
1 clove garlic
1 tablespoon pork fat
2 tablespoons olive oil
salt and pepper
a pinch of cayenne pepper
homemade bread

Trim and wash the chicory. Dry with a kitchen cloth. In a medium-sized nonstick pan, fry the garlic in the lard and olive oil. Discard the garlic when it begins to go brown. Throw in the raw chicory, and stir with a wooden spoon. Season with salt and pepper; add the cayenne pepper. Cook uncovered, adding, if necessary, a few tablespoons of water.

To keep it tasty, the chicory must stay soft, and is best enjoyed with thick slices of homemade bread.

PIUS IX

GIOVANNI MASTAI-FERRETTI

(1846–1878)

A cream puff for a good Pope

Archbishop Mastai-Ferretti's ecclesiastical career at Spoleto was not particularly auspicious: 1831 was a year of revolutions and interim governments; reports of the time tell of mild-mannered Giovanni fleeing on horseback from the Umbrian town on Palm Saturday, bound for the mountains where the border lay with the Kingdom of Naples. He stayed overnight at a convent, and then stopped at the Ceselli Tavern on the Nera River, where he drank a glass of fine wine before, setting off with the innkeeper's son as his guide, he headed on toward Leonessa.

Traveling through the barren mountains, he asked for something to drink from an old woman who lived in a hovel, and slaked his thirst with water from a spring, drinking from a grime-encrusted vessel; on he went as far as the Capuchin convent, where he was welcomed with open arms. They kindly refreshed him with a glass of rosolio liqueur and a tray of pastries which His Eminence enjoyed beyond all measure. The first pastry he picked from the tray was a *bignè* (cream puff), his favorite dessert, and for a moment he forgot all about the threat of the revolutionaries. The following morning, after a good night's sleep, he learned that his pursuers, the Romagnoli, had decided to turn back. He heaved a sigh of relief and began the journey home. For a short while he could live his life in peace. Alas, it was not to be for long. The situation had deteriorated even further by the time he was appointed Bishop of Imola, for he suffered the indignity of being "requisitioned." A certain Farini, who boasted that he had taken three cardinals hostage (Cardinal Mastai-Ferretti, Falconieri, Cardinal-Archbishop of Ravenna, and Amat, Legate Cardinal), only released them after the Pope granted an amnesty for political prisoners (1843).

Although holding beliefs that appealed to the moderate Liberals, after his election to pontiff on June 16, 1846, under the name Pius IX the former Cardinal Mastai-Ferretti always had to steer a course between a rock and a hard place, and to his dismay was more often than not fighting a rearguard action. By this time there was very little the archconservative Church could do to stem the revolutionary tide of the patriots.*

Brought up in Senigallia, in a minor noble family where, according to Gregory XVI, "even the cats were Liberals," this Pope found it hard to reconcile his open-mindedness with his high responsibilities as protector of the faith and of the state

* Sympathizers with the new Liberal/Democratic option for Italy got very close to the Pope. It is said that one day, just outside Mentana, the palace chefs dared to alter the decoration on a dessert—lots of black coffee beans, looking like priests wallowing around in the sponge-cake fingers steeped in strong coffee, custard and whipped cream—with the addition of a large red strawberry. When the noble diner asked what this innovation was for, he was told that the strawberry represented the heroic heart of Garibaldi, which remained forever in Rome.

against the Liberal and Masonic front which was striving to establish an Italian republic.

In the early months of his pontificate, he sent his troops to help King Charles Albert of Sardinia, known unkindly as Re Tentenna ("King Ditherer"), only to recall them very quickly, having realized that the new ideologies would end up in conflict with the Church. He panicked and opted for a policy of containment, and by the end of his long and dramatic pontificate (including his flight to Gaeta in 1848, proclamation of the Roman republic, and the beheading of two patriots in Rome in 1868), he had become the most hawkish of conservatives.

This is why, perhaps a little unfairly, so many historians have judged Pius IX to be a timid, vacillating and weak-willed pontiff. With the exception of the radical Liberals, however, the people thought him a kind Pope. Even Belli, so quick to criticize, had this to say:

Pè bono è bono assai; ma er troppo è troppo.
E accussi, tra l'ancudine e'r martello,
Se lassa persuade a annà berbello
E quer c'ha da fà pproma a fallo doppo.

(Good, yes he is good, but enough is enough.
And so, between a rock and a hard place,
He allows himself to be led along
And what he wanted to do, he leaves till later.)

Biographers acknowledge his wide-ranging culture, kind heart and sense of humor. He loved riding, even on his own; until the end of his days, as an old and frail man, he went for rides on a mule, which the stablemen saddled up and left for him at a certain place in the Vatican Gardens. The Holy Father climbed up two stone steps to make mounting the animal easier. He went for a little ride and then went back to his rooms to continue his regular and regulated existence.

He was in the habit of rising early; he spent the whole morning attending to pontifical offices, and then at two o'clock sharp broke for lunch. His meals tended to be frugal but of high quality: good man of the Marches that he was, Pius IX never lost his appetite.

Following a habit he had picked up from his family, he also insisted on an elegant and well-laid table. His menus, though, tended to be repetitive: risottos, Roman *fritto misto* (a tasty dish of unabashedly popular origins) and usually finishing with a cream puff or a slice of fruit tart. He would always have a glass of fine claret, perhaps in silent tribute to his allies, the French.

Pope Pius IX spent the afternoon reading or studying. After prayers, he adjourned for dinner. Once again, he ate simply: vegetable soup or broth with pasta, and a dish of seasonal vegetables, either raw or cooked. Once again, a glass of Bordeaux, this time white.

Perhaps it was this evening ration of vegetables that kept him in good health. As a child, Pius IX had suffered epileptic fits; as Pope he enjoyed the best of health and, though his position was so often hanging in the balance, presiding as he did over the major upheavals of Italy's Risorgimento (the establishment of Italy's first republic, the restoration, the taking of Porta Pia, declaration of Rome as national capital), he nevertheless played the long game and succeeded in modernizing the Pontifical State and Rome. It was thanks to him that a railway was built out to the Castelli. And when he traveled to Frascati, which he still sometimes did in his traditional carriage, he spent time with the crème de la crème of Roman society, the Bourbons of Naples, and the Infanta of Portugal.

Pius IX, who to his chagrin was accompanied everywhere by a large retinue, was unable to find peace and quiet even on holiday. Many of his holidays were altogether too eventful. His 1855 jaunt through the piazza at Rocca di Papa was ominously spoiled by the warning sign of a red hat sitting high in a tree, symbolizing the coming republic. Despite the glorious sunsets and relaxing rides, his 1865 holiday saw him grappling with French diplomats and the atheist Ideville. Christmas 1863 saw French and papal troops fighting it out among themselves, and on this occasion the Pope narrowly escaped death in what was a major diplomatic incident. There was always something happening; in some quarters it was believed that the good Pope, whose faith and moral integrity were unquestioned, was simply jinxed. A great deal of circumstantial evidence seemed to support this theory: bolts of lightning struck his carriage and the tents where he was holding Mass; bandits swelled the ranks of his procession; stray bullets or fireworks struck the Loggia at Castel Gandolfo with alarming regularity; stewards who glanced at him fell over holding their trays, at one reception covering the Pope in a large quantity of lemon sorbet.

Whatever the case, Pius IX always relied on circumspection and diplomacy to get him out of a fix. He greeted misfortune with his trademark good humor and was perhaps more astute than people give him credit for. Not only did he pray for Cavour's soul because he liked him, and because the man had done much good for the poor, but between one uprising and the next this Pope achieved many important things for the Church: he abolished the ancient ceremony of Jewish subjection, and opened the gates of the ghetto, an act of tolerance and modernity; he also proclaimed the dogma of the Immaculate Conception (1854) and commissioned construction of the Piazza di Spagna obelisk; in a solemn ceremony he consecrated the Church of San Paolo Fuori le Mura; and he celebrated the Jubilee year of 1867. He even succeeded in slightly improving the finances of the state after it plunged into a terrible crisis and suffered food-rationing in 1847; he also oversaw modernization of the Eternal City by installing gas lights and steam buses, to the wonderment of the people of Rome. He was responsible for introducing a ministry made up of lay and ecclesiastical members, and ushered in freedom of the press and a constitution.

Pius IX, the kindly Pope who was an enemy of war, lived through a great deal during his pontificate. He closed his eyes for good in his low and simple bed, raised above the ground on bare bricks, on February 7, 1878. His wish was to be buried in a plain stone sarcophagus in the Church of San Lorenzo Fuori le Mura. While he was being transported to this church, the pontifical guards risked their lives to rescue his corpse from the anger of a crowd of rabid anticlericals, who stoned the cortege and threatened to throw his remains into the Tiber.

✠

A menu for Pius IX.

BORDEAUX RISOTTO

✠

Ingredients for 4
1 onion, finely chopped
2 tablespoons olive oil
4 tablespoons butter
1 cup rice
1 glass of white Bordeaux wine
2-3 cups chicken stock, simmering
1 glass of heavy cream
salt and pepper to taste
1 tablespoon butter
4 tablespoons grated Parmesan cheese

Fry the onion in the oil and butter in a nonstick frying pan with high sides. Add the rice, stirring and cooking for a minute or two until it becomes transparent. Pour in the wine, and allow to evaporate, stirring all the while with a wooden spoon. Continue cooking, adding the stock little by little, making sure you continue to stir with the wooden spoon. Just before the rice is done, incorporate the cream. Season with salt and pepper. Remove from the heat; add the butter and half of the Parmesan cheese. Spread the steaming hot risotto into a serving dish and sprinkle over the rest of the Parmesan.

ROMAN-STYLE FRITTURA MISTA

✠

Frittura (which can be loosely translated as "fry-up") is a typical Roman dish that follows one of two possible forms: one version is typical of less well-off families and is served in the city's most basic trattorias, and consists of a few pieces of breaded beef, lamb or veal, almost always accompanied by fried vegetables coated in batter, typically cauliflower, zucchini, artichoke stems, apples and potato croquettes; the other version is the Grand Roman *frittura*, a more refined dish made up of thc ingredients listed below.

Ingredients for 6

2 pounds lamb's or veal brains, sweetbreads, and saddle
salt
a few drops of lemon juice
1 tablespoon olive oil
1 teaspoon chopped parsley
flour
3 eggs, beaten
pepper
4 cleaned artichokes, quartered and placed in lemon juice
a few slices of stale bread
pepper and salt to taste

Rinse the meat under running water, then boil for a few minutes in a small saucepan to which you have added a little salt. Drain, arrange on a kitchen towel and carefully remove the external skin, then cut into pieces roughly 1½ inches in diameter. Place in a bowl and dress with the lemon juice, oil and parsley. Dredge each piece of meat through the flour and then dip into the egg, which you have seasoned with salt and pepper. Fry the meat. When it is nice and brown, remove and place on kitchen paper. Lastly, arrange on a warm serving dish and garnish with the slices of bread, fried a golden brown color, and with *supplì* (rice croquettes) or the artichokes, fried in batter.

BIGNÈ ALLA CREMA

(CREAM PUFF WITH CUSTARD)

✠

Pius IX's favorite dessert, tasty and sophisticated, also used in other recipes (for example profiteroles).

Ingredients
1 cup water
a pinch of salt
8 tablespoons butter
1 tablespoon sugar
1 cup all-purpose flour
4 eggs

Bring the water to the boil, then add the salt, butter and sugar. Add all the flour at once, remove the saucepan from the heat and stir vigorously. Return the pan to the heat and stir until the mixture comes away from the sides of the pan and forms a ball. Off the heat once more, add the eggs, one at a time, stirring with a wooden spoon until the liquid is absorbed.

Work the mixture for at least 10 minutes, and then put through a pastry bag to make little heaps of pastry on a buttered baking sheet. Bake at 350°F for 40 minutes. After the puffs have cooled, use a pastry bag to fill them with custard, Chantilly cream, whipped cream, zabaglione, etc.

ROSOLIO

✠

And to finish off, a traditional liqueur with the sweet savor of rose petals, reputedly invented by a doctor from Padua called Michele Savonarola (fourteenth to fifteenth century).

Ingredients

1 cup honey

5 cups fragrant rose petals (or a few drops of rose oil, available at health food stores)

1 quart clear spirit

Pour the honey, rose petals and alcohol into a wide-mouthed bottle. Hermetically seal, shake well and then leave the liquid to steep in a cool, dark place.

One month later, filter the liquid, decant into a bottle and then leave for another 2 months. This drink makes an excellent accompaniment to desserts.

LEO XIII

VINCENZO GIOACCHINO
PECCI

(1878–1903)

An unpretentious little wine and fritters

When Leo XIII opened the Jubilee of 1900, he raised the curtain on the twentieth century, an era of radical social and political change, and of countless inventions that have irremediably altered the way we live—electricity, the telephone, the radio. . . . This ninety-year-old white-haired pontiff was so frail and delicate that people were concerned he would keel over beneath the weight of the heavy gold and silk vestments he had to wear for the opening ceremony at the Holy Door on December 24, 1899. To make sure this did not happen to him, some nuns made him an extra-light cloak which weighed little more than a veil. Old and tired he may have been, but in his reedy voice he proclaimed the year of *perdonanza*, touching the hearts and minds of the whole world.

Un uomo che quando fievole
mormori il mondo t'ode
pallido eroe, celeste, dell'Alto Atrio di Dio.

(A man who even when he weakly
murmurs, is heard by the world;
pale, heavenly hero, from God's Far Halls.)

wrote Giovanni Pascoli in his poem *La Porta Santa.*

Weak he may have been, but this pontiff was a real fighter. He took the brave step of inaugurating a Holy Year seventy-five years after the previous one, in a nation that, to all appearances, had become a lay society; he attempted to loosen the tight chains of the *Guarentigie*,* proving himself a man of strength, a man who wanted to restore the Church to politics after the end of its temporal authority.

Here we only have very limited scope to outline the history of the Church during the delicate and difficult period spanned by Leo XIII's pontificate. Many illustrious scholars have already achieved this task, debating, assessing, comparing and judging this great Pope and his role in making the tormented transition from the old century to the new. Our task is, rather, the less onerous one of seeking out the less familiar, more intimate yet no less significant—indeed perhaps indispensable—sides of his character in order to create a rounded picture of a person who left his mark on the history of Italy and all of Europe, not just in the field of religion.

He was born into a noble family near Rome (Carpineto Romano, March 2, 1810). We prefer to reveal his hidden side: he was something of a country gentleman, a lover of hunting, nature, flowers and vineyards, as we see not so much through documents from the official Vatican archives, but rather via the sincere, affectionate recollections of minor characters such as gardeners, gamekeepers and vine-dressers.

These were the people who shared private moments with

* Laws passed by the Italian Parliament in 1871, after the taking of Rome (1870), to guarantee a number of rights to the pontiff.

him when, briefly sheltered from the insistent callings and commitments of his position, the Pope came down from his throne and put the tiara to one side, and could chat good-naturedly about vines, the pheasants flying overhead, the best moment to sow seeds, and harvest time. We learn that "Sor Cesare," his chief gardener, often strolled along with him, and that they talked about work to be done in the garden, market garden and vineyard. Sometimes His Holiness had to be called to order because he could not resist the temptation to pick flowers, and therefore unbalance the fragrant and colored harmony of the flowerbeds.

The two men did not see eye to eye about running the vineyard, the great passion of the Pope, believing as he did that he could create a masterpiece of wine-making right on the Vatican Hill. To this end, he imported rare vine stock from distant countries, along with the best that the Bordeaux region had to offer. Leo XIII used to meet up with "Sor Cesare" in the vineyards for heated discussions about pruning, grafting, spraying with copper sulphate and all those seasonal operations that go to make up the triumph of the grape harvest. And woe betide anybody who dared to touch a bunch of grapes before harvest time. The Pope was so protective of his grapes that he had a fence put around the vineyard and a big gate and padlock installed!

But this putative masterpiece only caused him heartbreak. This special, well-tended and most blessed model vineyard produced a truly unremarkable little wine with a dry taste, not a patch on the wines drunk every day by the people of Rome. When His Holiness proudly offered it round the usual family gatherings at carnival time, served with the traditional fritters, everybody sang the wine's praises, knowing they were lying through their teeth. Afterward, in exchange, the flattered Pope gave his relatives a special bottle of excellent Bordeaux wine, sent for his personal consumption from France and of which, on the express orders of his doctor, he was supposed to drink a few sips as part of his otherwise sober, indeed very strict, diet.

As he never tired of telling people, Leo XIII did not suffer the sin of gluttony. He ate little and was very abstemious. There was no formal ritual surrounding his attitude to food: lunch, which was always a little meat served with vegetables, was served simply on a tray set on a folding table. In the evenings, for dinner, he asked for leftovers, reheated or cold, he didn't mind. Just after his election (February 20, 1878), in the euphoric post-conclave atmosphere, his trusted valet Baldassarri (who had served him since Perugia, where he previously served as bishop), to mark his first lunch as pontiff, dared to ask the chef to insert refined and unusual dishes into the daily menu, breaking the iron rules of his master's diet. For his troubles, Baldassarri received a severe reprimand: "If I have been made Pope, it's certainly nothing to do with my stomach." The poor valet canceled his noble selection of pontifical delicacies and, disconsolate, came back with the usual little tray with the usual slice of meat and boiled vegetables! Only a slice of cake every now and then, or a spitful of roast birds, ever broke this dietary rigor. But this latter gastronomical transgression was part and parcel of his other great passion, his love of hunting.

The Pope owned an old Belgian-made shotgun, a gift that

reminded him of his nunciature in Brussels, an important time during his career when he honed his abilities as an attentive observer and skilled communicator, creating quite a name for himself in European diplomatic circles. Obsolete it may have been, but the gun was extremely accurate, and His Holiness personally looked after it, making sure it was well oiled, housed in its case, and locked away in its small cupboard. Like all hunters, he never let anybody touch his gun, except, on rare occasions, his most trusted of Noble Guards, a man called Cecchini, who shared the Pope's passion for hunting. Cecchini was sometimes sent out with the precious pontifical shotgun to shoot the little birds that, were invading his beloved vineyards—birds which, despite being rather poor game, had the honor of winding up roasted on the Pope's table.

As we have observed, the Pope ate like any prelate, perhaps even more modestly than certain jolly curates in villages around Rome!

Though we have dwelt on his less solemn characteristics, this Pope was responsible for a sea change in the Catholic Church. Although he had been born in the early 1800s, his intuition about the social issues of the new century, and his farsightedness, made him one of the most important Popes in history. His words in the *Rerum Novarum** encyclical, and his actions during the Jubilee of 1900, showed that the

* *Rerum Novarum* ("Of New Things"): an encyclical of May 15, 1891, tackling the issue of workers with an outspoken spirit leaning toward socialism, and deep solicitude regarding the appalling living conditions of the "proletariat," along with a request for the state to intervene in such matters. This encyclical is considered the commencement of the Catholic Church's social doctrine.

cannonballs that had destroyed Porta Pia when Rome was taken had done nothing to undermine the Church's faith and spiritual authority.

In an increasingly secular Rome, of course, Pasquino could not remain silent:

Femo la pace Padre Santo
Quello ch'è stato è stato . . . qua la mano
E aringraziamo tutti quanti Iddio.

(Let's make peace, Holy Father
What's done is done . . . let's shake hands
And all give thanks to God.)

SOLE WITH ALMONDS, LEO XIII STYLE

✝

A mouthwatering recipe for sole cooked to golden perfection in oil and sprinkled with almonds would appear to clash with the image of strict Pope Leo. This recipe is proudly prepared by the chef at the Hôtel des Courriers in Troyes, a town on the banks of the Seine, in the French region of Champagne.

According to local gastronomical legend, apostolic nuncio Gioacchino Pecci, the future Pope, stopped here on his way to Brussels and particularly enjoyed the dish, which is the town's culinary pride and glory.

Here is the recipe, which we imagine was washed down with that most excellent of local wines—champagne.

Ingredients for 6

6 sole
salt and pepper
3 tablespoons flour
2 tablespoons oil
juice of 2 lemons
6 tablespoons butter
2 cups almonds (half bitter, half sweet)

Clean and rinse the sole. Sprinkle with salt and pepper and dredge in flour. Place in a large frying pan in which the oil is hot but not yet smoking. Brown the fish on both sides, turning just once during cooking (5–6 minutes). Drain the oil from the pan, without removing the sole, sprinkle them with lemon juice, then transfer to a warmed serving dish and keep warm. In the same pan, melt the butter, add the almonds and sauté using strong heat until golden. Season with salt and pepper, and pour this sauce over the sole. Serve immediately.

CARNIVAL FRITTERS

✞

To celebrate, with Pope Leo and his questionable little wine, there's nothing better than these fritters, made with leavened dough, a typical Lazio speciality.

Ingredients

6 cups all-purpose flour
1½ tablespoons dry yeast (or bread-starter dough)
a pinch of salt
half a glass of water
fine sugar
plenty of oil for frying

In a mixing bowl, use your fingers to blend together the flour, yeast and salt, gradually adding the water. Work the dough for 20 minutes or so. The mixture should be elastic and velvety, and come away from your hand and the bowl all in one piece. Cover the dough with a kitchen cloth and leave in a warm place for 5 hours.

Heat plenty of oil in a frying pan until it just starts to smoke. At this point, begin frying the fritters prepared in the following manner: using fingers moistened slightly with water, tear off pieces of dough the size of walnuts; arrange on a plate and, using your fingers, spread out each piece as wide as possible. When you drop these pieces of pastry into the pan they will shrink slightly before puffing up. Drain the nicely browned and crunchy fritters and serve immediately, heaped up in a serving dish. Sprinkle with fine sugar, or vanilla sugar if you prefer.

JOHN XXIII

ANGELO RONCALLI

(1958–1963)

A cup of warm broth for the Second Vatican Council

It was actually a cup of warm broth that comforted "*er Papa bono*" (the kindly Pope, as the people of Rome immediately nicknamed John XXIII) when, during one of the coldest Sundays in the winter of 1959, on a pastoral visit to the Abbey of San Paulo Fuori le Mura, he announced the holding of the Second Vatican Council to an improvised and amazed consistory of astonished, scarlet-clad prelates. Nobody expected such a bold move from this old man of seventy-seven, elected only three months previously, almost by chance, from a conclave (lasting three days, and requiring twelve votes) beset by uncertainties; the cardinals who voted for him did so in the hope that his would be a calm, transitional papacy after the long and solemn pontificate of Pius XII.

Sitting a little uncomfortably on a throne that was too stiff and imposing for him, Pope John, the man who had captivated and won friends the whole world over with the spontaneous manner of a country priest, and who somebody, in a hiss, had damned with the faint praise of being "modest," uttered nine hundred portentous words (punctiliously counted!), despite the fact that he was out of breath and his heart was beating in his ears, in the midst of one of the oldest Christian communities in the world.

Opposite sat seventeen stony-faced and dumbfounded cardinals. Refreshed by that cup of piping hot broth "because he felt all cold," he laid out his exceedingly well-planned and innovative idea of how to prepare the Church for the twenty-first century. Pope John's words gave voice and substance to the pressing need for renewal within the Church, not only to promote the spiritual well-being of Christian people, but also to bring together the separate communities and, by achieving long hoped-for unity, cement an ecumenical desire for peace on earth.

But who was this elderly Pope who wanted to commit himself to such a huge undertaking, a universal enterprise the like of which the Church had not dared to embark upon for so long?

The previous council had been called by Pius IX in 1870, only to be broken up by the occupation of Rome. Since then plenty of water and historical events had passed under the bridges on the Tiber. Now it was up to him, Pope John, this kindly grandfather figure with an easygoing and reassuring air, a man immediately accepted by all men, to initiate this epoch-making, almost revolutionary global venture.

This pontiff was immediately taken to the hearts of the people gathered in St. Peter's Square. Right after his election, he appeared before them to give his first *Urbi et Orbi* blessing on October 28, 1958. He came from Venice, for centuries the gateway to the world. There, as a patriarch, he had won the affections of the people not just for his good nature, but above all for his intelligent pastoral work, and the way he took part in everyday life on the city's streets.

But John XXIII's human journey began a little farther

north, in the hills around Bergamo, at a village called Sotto il Monte. Born in the last years of the nineteenth century, he came from a hale, modest and exemplary family of farmers, in which the head of the family, on winter evenings by the fireside, read out loud to his children the lives of the saints and excerpts from the Gospels. This patriarchal family numbered almost thirty souls, adults and children, who made a living from tilling the land; they were not destitute, but there were evenings when the future Pope had to share his dinner, an egg, with one of his brothers. This family, with its strong but understated affection, its atavistic rectitude and ancestral attachment to the earth and to God, was something that Pope John always carried with him like a deep and reassuring root; it was the source of a faith strong enough to lead him anywhere—as far as the Vatican, and even as far as heaven.

After he was elected, he was asked what name he would choose as pontiff. He replied, "*Vocabor Johannes*" (I shall be called John), a rare name in Vatican nomenclature (the last John XXIII had been an anti-Pope!),* and without a moment's hesitation, added, "It's my father's name!" And so, before that of his Precursor,† before the name of the Evangelist, the conclave heard the name of "Bergamo farm-laborer Giovanni Battista Roncalli, head of a peasant family where the men, the fathers, make their children into Christians." Everywhere he went, from the seminary in Bergamo to the Vatican halls, via First World War trenches, and apostolic posts

* Baldassarre Cossa (1410–1415).

† St. John the Baptist.

in Bulgaria, Turkey, France and Venice, Angelo Roncalli took along with him, like propitiatory divinities or custodian angels, portraits of his parents dressed in their Sunday best, taken by the village photographer. It was his parents, the way they passed on their straightforward and lofty conception of what it meant to live life as a Christian, who guided and supported him even during difficult moments when, among hostile nations, he needed to feel secure in his commitment and judgment.

One such moment was during the Second World War, when as apostolic nuncio to Istanbul, he put his own life at risk putting his signature to countless fake baptism certificates to save the life of many poor Jews who would otherwise have been exterminated by Nazi savagery; his heart and mind may well have been full of an image of a tableful of festive children, tucking into the polenta, in the big kitchen at home in Sotto il Monte.

On another occasion, in contravention of all the usual time-honored rituals, he wanted to spend his first Christmas as Pope visiting the prison at Regina Coeli, mingling (and not just in a figurative sense, as shown by the photos taken by the press that day) with the prisoners, including the most dangerous inmates with the longest sentences. Despite the concerns of the prison guards and his own security detail, with his own hand he gave them hope and a little comfort; he let them know that he was with them by recounting the sad tale of one of his relatives who wound up behind bars, sowing consternation among the family community.

Pope John XXIII's special way of bridging distances, of communicating directly with everybody, anybody, be they men of state with their hands on the wheels of power, or prisoners, or employees of the Vatican offices when he asked them about their pay, inevitably revealed his simple and even-tempered manner, which made him so popular and beloved the world over. Everybody became familiar with his typical little gestures, such as adjusting the skullcap on his head, his unmistakable and paternal smile, and the way he held out his hand; his reticence in using the *plurale maiestatis* (the royal we), his speeches, often beginning with an austere "we" and ending with an "I," immediately created an atmosphere of affectionate intimacy with the people who were listening to him, whoever they were.

People were interested to learn that in the frescoed Vatican halls the Holy Father continued his simple way of life, dedicating his early morning hours to study and prayer, and turning in for bed early in the evening, immediately after the television news. The world found out that immediately after the conclave the pontifical tailors busied themselves letting out the sacred vestments to accommodate Pope John's stout figure, and that in the gleaming kitchens, sisters of the order of St. Francis of Assisi from Bergamo prepared dishes from local peasant tradition for him, as they had done at home for their fathers and brothers: vegetables with a little meat, occasionally cheese such as Taleggio or Robiola, and, sometimes, extravagant and delicious cheeses sent from France by friends who remembered the tastes of apostolic nuncio Angelo Roncalli. But the Pope's ultimate moment of gustatory nostalgia, with its baggage of memories, history and life experience, was when the golden-yellow polenta arrived, as it did regularly, from the Bergamo countryside, in white canvas sacks. Before the empty sacks were returned to sender, the cornmeal was turned into a magical, steaming version of sunlight, shining on the table of a very noble peasant Pope.

Pope John would have liked to invite everybody to share his meal, old fellow seminarians who came timidly to visit, brimful with admiration, priests who once in their lives had been received by him, cardinals and foreign bishops who traveled from all over the world, prompted by the Council's ecumenical call, to Rome for the Vatican Council. But this could never be because, as everyone knows, the Pope eats alone! We are in no doubt that this weighed heavily upon him.

But in a figurative sense, this man did manage to bring together around his table the world's most powerful men, in one of the most difficult moments the modern age has lived through, when all it would have taken was a finger's pressure on a certain button and, in a flash, the human race would have been engulfed in the horrors of a new world war. It was Pope John who broke the bread of détente, as the world quaked in fear. Wielding unusual weapons for politics, such as the diplomacy of comprehension and dialogue, he graced even his enemies with his full and sincere attention. What followed was the gradual thaw of the Iron Curtain; after Khrushchev answered a simple Christmas goodwill message sent by the pontiff, an atmosphere was established that, in the end, was conducive to resolving the Cuban missile crisis, enabling John F. Kennedy, President of the United States, to go down in history as a man of peace, alongside Pope John XXIII.

"And now, my sons, I give you my blessing . . . and when you get home you will find the children. Give them an affectionate pat on the head and tell them: this pat is from the Pope."

These gentle words were the last he uttered on October 11, the long opening session of the Second Vatican Council. Pope John only saw the beginning of business, for he passed away on June 3, 1963. His work and his commitment have been admirably taken forward by Paul VI and John Paul II.

PAPAL POLENTA

✝

The culinary heritage of Bergamo and its surrounding area, so dear to Pope Roncalli's heart, is built mainly upon extremely simple dishes whose tastes and history are steeped in tradition. The Republic of Venice, which ruled the area for over three hundred years, left its mark in the form of polenta, made from corn left to dry in the sun on the plant, and then further sun-dried on the threshing floor before being milled into cornmeal. Traditionally, the corn was stone ground in such a fashion as to produce *farina bramata,* without destroying or heating up the corn. A real gift of God, polenta is often served with the freshest milk, and somehow carries with it a faint whiff of shepherds' huts (the famous Roman chef Apicius knew all about this); it is also excellent with wild mushrooms, game, salamis and either soft or strong cheeses.

Ingredients

4 cups water
½ pound coarse-ground cornmeal
a pinch of salt

Bring the water to the boil in a copper pot (ideally you suspend the pot above a wood fire). Add salt. Sprinkle in the cornmeal, stirring continuously. This hail of meal must come down gently so that it does not form lumps which are hard to break down. Once all the meal is in the pot, you should stir more vigorously.

In the late nineteenth century and early twentieth century, polenta was used instead of bread, as a base for spreads and toppings.

Polenta with Milk—Piping hot polenta and cold milk was the traditional midday meal for country folk.

Polenta "Cunsa"—Dressed polenta was spooned out of the copper pot and served in a big bowl with melted butter aromatized with garlic and grated cheese.

Polenta "Rostida"—Roast polenta was cold polenta cut into slices and grilled in a frying pan in which onion had softened in butter.

Polenta "Pastizzata"—Layered polenta pie with tomatoes, the big dish for special occasions: alternate layers of polenta, tomato sauce, sausage, minced pork and mushrooms cooked in a baking pan, finishing with the tomato sauce and grated cheese. Baked for half an hour or so.

PAUL VI

GIOVANNI BATTISTA MONTINI

(1963–1978)

Italian Spumante to toast the continuation of the Second Vatican Council

One evening in November 1963, Pope Montini, a rather shy and mild-mannered Pope who hated upsetting others, invited the French philosopher Jean Guitton, a member of the Académie Française, the sole lay observer admitted to attend proceedings of the Second Vatican Council, to dinner at the usual time of 8:15 P.M., in the third loggia at the Vatican. Also invited along was the Pope's personal adviser, Monsignor Bevilacqua, who accompanied him fraternally throughout his long pontificate. They talked at length about French literature, with which Pope Montini was well acquainted; they talked of Bernanos and Sartre, of materialistic philosophies and theology, and the Pope, who some years earlier as a monsignor had been regarded as a revolutionary, for the first time uttered a full formulation of his concept of the papacy: that it had the power to bring together the different confessions, an idea that was alluring and bold, yet hard to achieve because of its newness. Toasting his friends with flutes full of sparkling Colli Bresciani wine, Paul VI laid out his game plan, the plan he would follow in the continuation of the Second Vatican Council, initiated by his predecessor (September 29, 1963). He announced his thinking in summary form that June on the radio, explaining that the council would look into renewal of Church doctrine, and rapprochement with all Christians, atheists and dissidents, Russia included.

And the Pope from Concesio, who as a child, despite a weak heart, loved climbing trees in the garden at his maternal grandparents' house in Verola Nuova, had an extremely ambitious plan in mind, which, when put into practice, aroused a great deal of dissent. His pontificate came at a time which could not possibly have been described as straightforward.

On one hand, he was keen to pursue the work begun by Pope John, whose faith and good cheer had won over the crowd; at the same time, he wished to slow down the pace of change—so often piecemeal, and sometimes at the very limits of orthodoxy—that was sweeping through the Church, prompted by a society in the midst of an economic boom, consumed by materialistic thoughts and consumerism, and wracked by the 1968 uprisings and radical goings-on that were altering the way the most advanced societies were structured.

It was not easy for Pope Montini, formerly apostolic nuncio to Warsaw, student at the Vatican Ecclesiastical Academy, Secretary of State, Archbishop of Milan appointed by Pius XII, a committed antifascist and a rather inconvenient priest because of his open-mindedness toward all forms of culture and freedom. All this taught him that dialogue was the only way to resolve disputes.

Dressed in a perfectly fitting beige-colored tunic and red babouches, and with his inimitably elegant way of doing things, a pensive expression in his gray eyes, he set himself the task of talking over every issue, the most problematic areas of the faith, such as Pentecost and morality, honing his ideas with lay intellectuals such as his French friend Guitton, and monks of every confession.

Despite the high rank of his office, he did not consider it beneath himself to seek advice from his friends, often over a dinner in the third loggia.

Invitations from the Pope were a bolt from the blue, taking his guests by surprise. They were often a little embarrassed and fearful of such a high-ranking invitation, but always found themselves soon put at ease.

They discussed major issues until late, over simple but quite elegant meals. Indeed, Pope Montini still adhered to the gentlemanly habits of his upbringing in an affluent family in Brescia (one of his brothers was an Italian senator). By way of example, the following dishes were served at dinner on the evening of fasting before the feast of All Souls in 1970: soup with rice, brains in lemon, mashed potatoes and vegetables, and marrons glacés. The Pope had asked to end the meal with a dessert from his own birthplace, a hearty peasant winter dessert, very tasty, made from almonds, spices, Marsala wine and flour, which, as he informed his friends, was known in his village as *scheletri* (skeletons), but which people commonly referred to as *Ossa di morto* (dead man's bones).

Despite the upheavals of his pontificate and his own unstinting work, particularly on countless trips around the world, taking in Bombay, the Holy Land, the United States, Bogotà (and including an assassination attempt in Manila in 1976, as well as stones thrown at him in Cagliari six years earlier), Paul VI never forgot the warmth of the home he grew up in, the green Po Valley plain, the freshness of its hills, and the beauty of its lakes. In remembrance of all this, he sometimes asked the chef, particularly when he was at Castel Gandolfo, on certain September days when the air had a crispness to it, to make him and his friends the famous Brescian dish of polenta and *osei*, a humble yet tasty meal made with sparrows, blackbirds, or at most quails.

Another dish that at least invokes small birds, without actually serving them up, is "flown" birds (*uccelletti scappati*), a splendid tasty dish usually reserved for the Sunday meal in the Lombardy region: a veal rump roulade containing a slice of Parma ham and a cube of Parmesan cheese, sautéed in sage butter and flavored with white wine.

On evenings like this the Pope thought often of his original home. When he had occasion to sample the flavors of his homeland, he smiled tenderly, and his gray eyes looked wistfully into the distance. He spoke with his friends about his dear mother, his brothers and sisters, his father's clear-eyed death, and his own weak heart.

He said he was not afraid of death—it was something he had carried with him since childhood—nor of the feeling of precariousness to which, against his will, he had been forced to become accustomed. In fact, his wayward heart pulled through admirably, giving him moral strength and a great lifelong constancy.

On more than one occasion, Paul VI's openness to dialog, for example his meeting with the Soviet leader Podgorni, earned him accusations of being a Communist sympathizer.

His enormous faith, founded upon deep and extensive

learning, his tireless industry, allied with a spirit of sacrifice and humility (the very qualities he employed with the Red Brigade members who were holding Italian Prime Minister Aldo Moro hostage), enabled him to overcome his critics and see through a wide-ranging program of modernization and consolidation of the Catholic Church, while at the same time breaking brand-new ground (for instance, his condemnation of anti-Semitism and any form of racial discrimination).

For the Twenty-fifth Jubilee, celebrated in 1975, Pope Montini injected his own special focus on prayer and forgiveness, under the banner of ecumenism.

And yet in his personal life, the learned Montini was very much a man of the area where he grew up: industrious, solid and thoughtful. Every now and then, as he tucked in to a dish of polenta and *osei* at one of his palaces, his thoughts returned to those very same lands.

It has been said that at the very moment he passed away, a little Polish alarm clock he used, a souvenir of a distant journey, went off even though it had not been set for that hour. Happenstance, or a wake-up call from God?

POLENTA E OSEI

✠

Here is a recipe for a dish Pope Montini loved to eat every autumn at Castel Gandolfo, a tasty dish typical of the area where he grew up—an area of hunters and strong flavors.

Ingredients for 4
3 bay leaves
3 slices *pancetta*, cubed
4 pigeons without giblets, singed over a flame
1 white onion, sliced
oil
butter
salt and pepper
1 small glass of brandy
2 teaspoons tomato paste
1 ladle stock
polenta

Insert a piece of bay leaf and a little *pancetta* inside each little bird. Brown the onion in oil and butter in a high-sided frying pan. Throw in the pigeons, season with salt and pepper, then pour in the brandy. When it has partially evaporated, add the tomato paste and continue cooking with a ladleful of stock, making sure that there is a little sauce left at the end. Serve piping hot in a round serving dish, garnished with a fan-shape of toasted polenta sliced about ½ inch thick.

UCCELLETTI SCAPPATI

(FLOWN BIRDS)

✞

After the real little birds . . . fake ones. This delicate but flavorful dish uses typical ingredients from Lombard and Emilian cuisine: butter, Parmesan, and Parma ham.

Ingredients for 6

around 2 pounds thinly sliced and flattened veal rump
5–6 slices Parma ham
6 ounces Parmesan, cubed
4 tablespoons butter
4 sage leaves
salt and pepper
half a glass of dry white wine

On a cutting board, smooth out each slice of meat, and then place on each a slice of Parma ham and a cube of Parmesan cheese. Fold into a parcel and tie up with kitchen string. In a nonstick pan heat the butter until it foams, add the sage, and then carefully set down the "little birds." Carefully turn them using a wooden spoon. Season with salt and pepper, add the wine and, if necessary, a little water, then lower the heat and continue cooking (around 20 minutes). Serve hot, garnished with endive in butter, and mashed potato.

OSSA DI MORTO

(DEAD MAN'S BONES)

✠

This is the Lombard dessert Pope Montini was so partial to, typically eaten on All Souls' Day. It is as lugubrious as it is tasty.

Ingredients

1¼ cups peeled almonds, baked for a few minutes
a pinch of cinnamon
5 cloves
1 cup all-purpose flour, sifted
¾ cup sugar
glass of dry Marsala

Crush half the almonds into a powder in a mortar, along with the cinnamon and cloves. Blend together with the flour and sugar, using the Marsala to add liquid, taking care that the dough does not become too runny. Reserving a few for decoration, chop the remaining almonds into strips and add them to the dough. When the dough is well amalgamated, divide up into lots of small cylinders and place these on a buttered baking tray, leaving a little distance between them.

Place a few little strips of almond on each one, and push them gently into the dough. Bake in a fairly hot oven at 400°F for 25 minutes.

DRY PINOT DI FRANCIACORTA SPUMANTE

✝

Raise your glasses . . .

This wine is produced in the uplands that run toward Lake Iseo, between Brescia and Bergamo. Excellent for toasting, with dessert, and a fine accompaniment to sophisticated hors d'oeuvres, such as snails. This wine's old-fashioned name perhaps refers to medieval monks or to a French garrison stationed in this area in the eighteenth century (France-Court).

A white wine made from Pinot grapes, yellowish in color with green hints, dry, fruity, with delicate aromas. It is ready to drink one year after production, and reaches 11.5% alcohol. This wine is made in dry, reserve and sparkling versions.

JOHN PAUL II

KAROL WOJTYLA

(SINCE 1978)

From Kraków with love

In a recent televised interview General Martini, head of the secret services responsible for supervising John Paul II's many pastoral visits, admitted his fear that the Polish Pope might fall victim to poisoning. On one journey to Holland his retinue included a taster, a specialist chemist who could tell if the food put before the Pope had been tampered with.

Without doubt, Karol Wojtyla's long and event-filled pontificate, including the assassination attempt of 1981, has been extremely tough because of his unyielding desire for peace, ecumenism, and charity, which he has pursued with steadfastness and courage. Despite the strong opposition he has encountered along the way, his dedication has offered great hopes of freedom for humanity in the name of faith at every latitude.

It is not hard to imagine how much importance a man of such moral strength ascribes to food! But food is necessary to live. Between one plane trip and the next, the Pope eats light soups and drinks invigorating and thirst-quenching teas.

In his childhood he was brought up on simple foods; onion and cabbage soups warmed him up during those long, cold winters. Orphaned at a young age, as a young man he was forced to abandon his studies because of the fearsome German invasion of Poland. For a spell he worked in a Kraków factory, in his free time pursuing his interests in drama and sport (he was an accomplished skier and canoeist, and a goalkeeper too), as well as spending many hours praying; he became a prisoner and a priest, and never allowed himself to be worn down by the atrocity of the massacres, persecution and censorship. On the contrary, suffering strengthened his spirit, Christian faith and evangelical charity, something he applied directly in his daily attendance of working families whom he visited after their nearest and dearest had been killed.

Like all great Christians, the young Karol arrived at the faith through secular experience and courageous charity given without reserve to friends, workers and prisoners. In all likelihood it is this that has allowed John Paul II to know life in all of its high and low points; his ability to apply his active faith has allowed him to dismantle the barriers erected by man's brutality.

His writings in *Gift and Mystery,* an autobiographical memoir of his path toward the clarity of faith, are both lovely and illuminating. His early sufferings, his mother's death, the death of his brother and father, his time spent with working families whose love helped him to overcome every obstacle, the even-handed guidance of the Salesian Fathers, the example given by the Carmelites, his study of the mystics, his journeys in a cart with farmhands on his way to his first vicarship at Niegovic, the poor, rustic food eaten in Poland after the Nazi devastation, in which potatoes and onions were ever-present staples, all these were crucial steps along the way for this young parish priest who, unknowingly, had begun his journey to Peter's throne.

Immediately after his somewhat surprising election as Pope, following the sudden and some say obscure death of Pope John Paul I, he showed the faithful that he was a charming and smiling man, and wasted no time in applying his formidable will to the pursuit of specific objectives: dialogue with everyone, faithful and otherwise, Polish, American, Russian, African or Chinese. His ever-clear messages are built upon long years of philosophical and theological study (he took his doctorate in 1948 with a dissertation on St. John of the Cross, and qualified to lecture with a dissertation on Max Scheler); though of apparent simplicity, they are the result of study and meditation. His chosen points of focus became a struggle for ecumenism, improvement of the lot of women (perceived as bearers of life and the fulcrum of society), abolition of prejudice against Judaism, and the full rehabilitation of Galileo's thought, still hobbled by the actions of the Inquisition.

How is it possible to reconcile the prosaic nature of food with a life lived so intensely, even if he has been worn down by the deep wounds of the attempt on his life, and by the sufferings of old age, not to mention the cares which are always part and parcel of such high office?

The story of John Paul II still remains to be written—we hope, with all our hearts, as far in the future as possible. At present, as far as our own endeavors are concerned, despite our probings, very little has come to light about His Holiness' eating habits, beyond the fact that he eats simply.

His daily diet consists of soups, soft cheeses, white meat,

steamed vegetables and tea. The strong flavors of Polish cuisine are no longer suitable for an elderly Pope, though the three nun chefs, who come from his own land, do occasionally allow themselves a little free rein. As he shuttles from one time zone to the next, he has to keep his mind sharp and feed his typically ironic way of speaking. The full-bodied flavors of Italian cuisine can also sometimes be a little strong for him. We do know that on one trip to New York, where he ate at the Giambelli restaurant, he enjoyed *saltimbocca alla romana*, and that on a trip to Siena the Polish Pope forsook his usual cup of tea for a glass of Montalcino red wine.

All that remains is for us to toast his health, and the success of the Year 2000 Jubilee, which has been the focus of great preparations, including a special cake dedicated to the pontiff, made to a top-secret recipe devised by the Moroni pastry shop of Castel Gandolfo. The hope remains that this great feast of forgiveness and Christian hope can retain its deeper meaning. Whether or not this is the case, a nice slice of chilled watermelon will help to keep the pilgrims cool during their long waits, and the trattorias found in abundance inside and outside Rome will be rolling out their traditional menus. A country like Italy is proud of maintaining its culinary traditions, even if moderation is fitting for the penitent pilgrim. Who knows, perhaps Polish food will be popular during the Jubilee!

✠

Knowing that he would relish them, we dedicate to His Holiness a few recipes from his distant homeland.

POLISH-STYLE PIKE

Ingredients for 4

1 small spring onion, finely chopped

1 white onion, finely chopped

4 tablespoons oil

1 pike weighing roughly 2 pounds, gutted and descaled, then cut into chunks

1 glass of red cooking wine

1 glass of sour cream

salt

a pinch of paprika

4 hard-boiled eggs

2 tablespoons soaked large raisins

a few soaked and candied plums

Sauté the spring onion and onion in the oil. Add the fish and cook in the red wine. Before serving add the sour cream, salt and paprika, and mix, using a wooden spoon.

Make sure that the cream does not come to the boil. Arrange on a serving dish and garnish with slices of egg, raisins and plums. This dish is best served warm, accompanied by boiled potatoes, and makes a hearty meal on its own.

POLISH SAUCE

✟

A delicious sauce for boiled meat or fish.

Ingredients for 6

4 pounds finely grated white radish root
1 cup heavy cream
½ tablespoon caraway seeds
2 teaspoons lemon juice

Put the radish in a mixing bowl and add the cream. Stir with a wooden spoon until it is well amalgamated. Add the caraway seeds, blend well and then, just before serving, add the lemon juice, making sure that it is properly mixed.

THICK POLISH SOUP

✝

Ingredients for 6
a few tablespoons all-purpose flour
3 pounds finely filtered chicken or veal stock
1 cup cream
salt and pepper as necessary
small cubes of peeled cucumber, sprinkled with salt

In a nonstick saucepan dilute the flour in a little cold stock and cream, making sure that it does not form lumps. Add the rest of the cold stock. Bring to the boil, check the seasoning and then serve in china consommé cups. In each cup place a few cubes of cucumber. Serve piping hot.

BRUNELLO DI MONTALCINO

✝

To toast His Holiness.

Made from Brunello grapes in Montalcino (near Siena), this is a classic red wine ideal for meat dishes or mature cheeses. An intense ruby color, with a warm and dry taste and a characteristic nose, this wine reaches an alcoholic content of 12.5%, and is generally drunk between five and nine years after production. After aging for five years, it is known as reserve wine, and is one of Italy's greatest red wines.

PANE DELLA CARITÀ

CHARITY BREAD

✞

To conclude . . . stop-press news. A new type of bread has gone on sale in Italy. It is baked from a blend of equal parts of wheat, oat and barley flour. Light and crunchy, it is sold in round loaves and can be divided up into twelve portions (the apostles), plus a central raised medallion (Jesus). Income from sales will be donated to Third World nations.

BIBLIOGRAPHY

✟

Accolti, P. *Vini di Francia.* Rome: Newton Compton Editore, 1972.

Agasso, D. *Il Papa delle grandi speranze.* Milan: Editore Mondadori, 1967.

Alberini, M. *Storia della cucina italiana.* Casale Monferrato: Piemme Editore, 1992.

Alighieri, D. *La Divina Commedia.* Edited by N. Sapegno. Milan, 1979.

Andreotti, G. *La sciarada di Papa Mastai.* Milan: Rizzoli Editore, 1967.

Baracconi, G. *I rioni di Roma.* Rome: Napoleone Editore, 1976.

Bargellini, P. *Anno Santo.* Genoa: Marietti Editore, 1987.

Belli, G. *Sonetti romaneschi.* Edited by B. Caglia. Rome, 1980.

Benporat, C. *Storia della gastronomia europea.* Milan: Mursia Editore, 1990.

Besso, M. *Roma ed il Papa.* Florence: Editore Olschy, 1971.

Boccaccio. *Tutte le Opere, De mulieribus claris.* Milan: Mondadori, 1997.

Bockeneym, G. *La cucina di Martino V.* Edited by G. Bonardi. Milan: Mondadori Editore, 1995.

Boni, A. *La cucina romana*. Rome: Newton Compton Editore, 1998.

Bonomelli, E. *I Papi in campagna*. Rome: G. Casini Editore, 1997.

Bradford, S. *I Borgia*. Milan: Sperling e Kupfer Editore, 1992.

Brezzi, P. *Storia degli Anni Santi, da Bonifacio VIII al Giubileo del 2000*. Milan: Mursia Editore, 1997.

Buonassisi, V. *La cucina degli Italiani*. Milan: Idea Libri Editore, 1998.

Cardini, F. *Alla corte dei Papi*. Milan: Mondadori Editore, 1995.

Carugati, D. *La cucina dell'allegria*. Vigevano: Diacronia Editore, 1994.

Cattabiani, A. *Santi d'Italia*. Milan: Rizzoli Editore, 1992.

Chamberlin, E. R. *Ascesa e tramonto dei Borgia*. Milan, 1976. (English edition: *The Fall of the House of Borgia*. London: Temple Smith, 1974.)

Chiodi, E. *C'e qualcosa di nuovo oggi in cucina, anzi d'antico*. Milan: Acanthus Editore per Fabbri, 1990.

Consiglio-Frignani. *Il diavolo nel bicchiere*. Rome: Canesi Editore, 1968.

Da Varagine, J. *La leggenda aurea*. Florence: Libreria Fiorentina, 1994.

Di Corato, R. *Il bicchiere d'argento*. Domus Editore, 1968.

———. *Il gastronauta*. Milan: Sonzogno Editore, 1976.

Di Teodoro, F. *Ritratto di Leone X*. Milan: Tea Arte Editore, 1998.

Dorez, L. *La cova du Pape Paolo III*. Paris: 1993.

Escoffier, A. *Guida dalla grande cucina*. Trento: F.lli Muzio Editore, 1990. (English edition: *A Guide to Modern Cookery*. London: William Heinemann, 1933.)

Esposito, P. *I giubilei ieri ed oggi*. Udine: Segno Editore, 1997.

Et coquatur ponendo—Cultura della cucina e della tavola in Europa tra Medioevo ed età moderna. Prato: Istituto Internazionale di Storia Economica F. Datini di Prato, 1996.

Faccioli, F. *L'arte della cucina*. Turin: Einaudi, 1997.

Falconi, C. *I Papi del XX Secolo*. Milan: Feltrinelli Editore, 1963.

Ferri, E. *Io, Caterina*. Scie Mondadori. Milan, 1997.

Fischer, H. A.C. *Storia d'Europa*. Milan: Mondadori Editore, 1994.

Fo, D. *Le Commedie*. Turin: Einaudi Editore, 1997.

Gaudenzio, E. *Il Panunto Toscano*. Rome: Trevi Editore, 1974.

Giovanni Paolo II. *Dono e mistero*. Rome: Libreria Editrice Vaticana, 1996.

Gregorovius, E. *La storia dei Papi*. Rome, 1972.

Guitton, J. *Paolo II segreto*. Rome: Editore Paoline, 1981.

Jannatoni, L. *Osterie e feste romane*. Rome: Newton Compton Editore, 1991.

La Bella-Mecarolo. *La venere papale*. Vitterbo: Scipioni Editore, 1995.

Malizia, G. *La cucina ebraico romanesca*. Rome: Tascabili Newton Compton, 1997.

Mantovano, G. *La cucina italiana, origini, storia, segreti*. Rome: Newton Compton Editore, 1992.

Marchi, C. *Quando siamo a tavola*. Milan: Rizzoli Editore, 1990.

Massorbio, A. *La storia della Chiesa*. Rome: Newton Compton Editore, 1997.

Mignolli, L. *Il farro e le sue ricette*. Luca: Pacini-Fazzi Editore, 1992.

Mollat, G. *Les Papes d'Avignon*. Paris, 1995.

Montanari, M. *Il nuovo Convivio*. Bari: Laterza, 1991.

———. *La fame e l'abbondanza*. Bari: Laterza, 1997.

Paparelli, G. *Enea Silvio Piccolomini*. Bari: Laterza, 1960.

Paravicini, A. and A. Bagliani. *Vita quotidiana alla Corte dei Papi nel Duecento*. Bari: Laterza, 1995.

Pernaud, A. *I Santi nel Medioevo*. Milan: Rizzoli Editore, 1986.

Picco, C. *Dizionario gastronomico*. Edited by R. Gualandi. Bologna: Editore Fusconi, 1991.

Piccolomini, E. S. *Commentari*. Siena, 1972.

Pio X, Archbishop of Spoleto (1827–1832). *Atti del Convegno di studi storico ecclesiastici su "La figura e l'opera di Pio IX."* Florence: Vallecchi Editore, 1980.

Platina. *La vita dei Pontefici*. Venice, 1715.

Rendina. *I Papi, storia e segreti*. Rome: Newton Compton Editore, 1996.

Righi G. and Parenti. *II buon mangiare*. Siena: Al Saba Editore, 1996.

Sabban-Serventi. *A tavola nel Medioevo*. Bari: Laterza Editore, 1994.

———. *A tavola nel Rinascimento*. Bari: Laterza Editore, 1994.

St. Valentin, L. *La cocina de las mojnas*. Madrid: Alianza Editore, 1993.

Sarazani, F. *La Roma di Sisto V*. Rome: I Dioscuri, 1979.

Schiaffino, M. *Le ore del caffè*. Lainate: Idea Libri, Vallardi Editore, 1994.

Scotto, P. *Formaggi e vini d'Italia*. Rome: Gremese Editore, 1997.

Simone, P. M.C. Lacchi. *I peccati di gola*. Rome: Anthropos Editore, 1989.

Spadanuda, L. *La Papessa Giovanna*. Viterbo: Scipioni Editore, 1996.

Tenenti, A. *L'Italia nel Quattrocento*. Bari: Laterza Editore, 1996.

Tognazzi, U. *L'Abbuffone*. Milan: Rizzoli Editore, 1994.

Ullmann, W. *Il Papato nel Medioevo*. Bari, 1975.

Vaona, M. *Grandi vini italiani*. Milan, 1990.

Vasari, G. *Le vite dei più eccellenti pittori, scultori, architetti*. Rome: Newton Compton Editore, 1997.

Villani, G. *Cronache*. Florence, 1823.

Volponi, W and P. Verse. *La tavola d'oro*. Milan: Vallardi Editore, 1982.

Young, G. E. *I Medici*. Florence: Salani Editore, 1941.

Zanazzo, G. *Leggende e storie romane*. Rome: Meravigli Editore, 1992.

———. *Tradizioni popolari romane*. 2 vols. Tarquinia: La Bancarella Romana Editore, 1994.

Zanini, O. and D. De Vita. "A tavola con i Papi," *Il Lazio a Tavola*. Rome: Editore Assessorato al Turismo della Regione Lazio, 1990.

Zeppegno, L. *I rioni di Roma*. Rome, 1978.

RECIPE & WINE INDEX

GENERAL INDEX